PREFACE

In 1982 we conducted a survey of the use of planning agreements by planning authorities in Scotland. The results, which were published as a Scottish Planning Law and Practice Occasional Paper by the Planning Exchange, showed considerable interest by authorities in the use of such agreements but some uncertainty about the propriety of their use as a supplement to development control powers.

Land development during the intervening years has taken place against the background of a government programme designed to promote the primacy of the market place. This has manifested itself in continuing relaxation of statutory planning controls, in continuing restraint on public expenditure and in acquiescence in an increasing role for bargaining between local authorities and developers signalled in the advice contained in SDD Circular 22/1984 on the use of planning agreements. All three factors might be expected to contribute towards an increase in the use of agreements. Because of this we felt it appropriate, six years on, to conduct a further survey. We are grateful to local authority officers throughout Scotland for the time and trouble taken in supplying us with information. Part of this book is devoted to publication of our findings. These show, as expected, a considerable increase in the use of agreements over the intervening years and it is clear that planning by agreement is now widespread in Scotland.

The great majority of such agreements are entered into under section 50 of the Town and Country Planning (Scotland) Act 1972. This relatively short and apparently self-contained section gives rise to very considerable legal complexity and much of this book is given over to an examination of this complexity. Given the limited judicial scrutiny of this provision, some of what we say is inevitably of a somewhat speculative nature. The law is stated as at July 1, 1988.

The book is based on, and incorporates much of, the 1982 Occasional Paper. However, account has also been taken of current local authority practices in this area, of SDD Circulars 22/1984 "Section 50 Agreements" and 18/1986 "The Use of Conditions in Planning Permissions" and of recent court decisions, in particular, the Court of Appeal decisions in *Windsor and Maidenhead Royal Borough Council* v. *Brandrose Investments*

[1983] 1 W.L.R. 509 and *City of Bradford Metropolitan Council* v. *Secretary of State for the Environment* (1986) 53 P. & C.R. 55 and that of the Queen's Bench Division in *R.* v. *Gillingham Borough Council, ex p. F. Parham Ltd.* [1988] J.P.L. 336. We have also had regard to recent developments in law and practice relating to other statutory agreements which guide and control land use change, particularly those relating to the changing countryside.

The object of this book is to provide a reasonably comprehensive guide to the law and practice of planning by agreement in Scotland. It is directed principally at those with an interest in land development either as practitioners or students. As was said in the *Journal of the Law Society of Scotland* "it is . . . important (whether or not missives have been completed and whether or not the builder is under obligation to produce planning permissions or searches) to ascertain whether or not a section 50 agreement is in existence, and if so, what its terms are and whether they have been complied with by the builder" ((1981) 26 J.L.S. 464). We would add that this comment seems equally appropriate not just to new houses, but to existing houses and also to commercial, industrial and recreational property.

In writing this book we have incurred a debt of gratitude, not only to local authorities throughout Scotland, but to a number of other bodies and individuals, in particular, to the Countryside Commission for Scotland, the National Trust for Scotland and the Capital Taxes Office for supplying information, to Douglas Cusine of the Department of Conveyancing and Professional Practice of Law, and Louise Livingstone of the Department of Land Economy, both of Aberdeen University for comments on individual chapters, to Maureen Reid for her fortitude and endurance in typing much of the manuscript, and to our families for their patience. We are pleased to have this opportunity to thank them.

Jeremy Rowan-Robinson
Eric Young
1 July 1988

Planning by Agreement in Scotland

Planning by Agreement in Scotland

BY

JEREMY ROWAN-ROBINSON, M.A., LL.M.,
Senior Lecturer in Law, University of Aberdeen

AND

ERIC YOUNG, M.A., LL.B.,
Reader in Law, University of Strathclyde

EDINBURGH

W. GREEN & SON LTD.

2 ST. GILES STREET

GLASGOW

THE PLANNING EXCHANGE

186 BATH STREET

1989

First published in 1989

ISBN 0 414 00855 3

PRINTED IN GREAT BRITAIN BY
THE EASTERN PRESS LTD

CONTENTS

TABLE OF CASES

TABLE OF STATUTES

TABLE OF STATUTES

TABLE OF CIRCULARS

xvii

ABBREVIATIONS

1972 Act	The Town and Country Planning (Scotland) Act 1972.
1973 Act	The Local Government (Scotland) Act 1973.
C.A.	Court of Appeal.
D.A.F.s	Department of Agriculture and Fisheries for Scotland.
DoE	Department of the Environment.
General Development Order ...	The Town and Country Planning (General Development) (Scotland) Order 1981, as amended.
H.L.	House of Lords.
M.H.L.G.	Ministry of Housing and Local Government.
N.C.C.	Nature Conservancy Council.
P.A.N.	Planning Advice Note.
R.I.C.S.	Royal Institution of Chartered Surveyors.
R.T.P.I.	Royal Town Planning Institute.
S.D.D.	Scottish Development Department.
Use Classes Order	The Town and Country Planning (Use Classes) (Scotland) Order 1973, as amended.

Reference to *Scottish Planning Appeal Decisions* (SPADS) are references to the summaries of appeal decisions published by the Planning Exchange, Glasgow.

A.C. or 1 App.Cas.	Appeal Cases (Law Reports).
All E.R.	All England Law Reports.
Ch.	Chancery (Law Reports).
E.G.	Estates Gazette.
F.	Fraser (Court of Session, etc. reports 1898–1906).
J.L.S.	Journal of the Law Society of Scotland.
J.P.L.	Journal of Planning and Environment Law.
K.B.	King's Bench (Law Reports).
L.G.R.	Knight's Local Government Reports.
L.R.	Law Reports.
P. & C.R.	Property, Planning and Compensation Reports.
Ph.	Phillip's Reports (Chancery 1841–1849).
Q.B.	Queen's Bench (Law Reports).
R.	Rettie (Court of Session, etc., reports 1873–1898).
R.V.R.	Rating and Valuation Reporter.
S.C.	Session Cases (Court of Session, etc., reports).
S.J.	Solicitor's Journal.
S.L.T.	Scots Law Times.
S.L.T. (Lands Tr.)	Scots Law Times Lands Tribunal reports.
S.L.T. (Notes)	Scots Law Times Notes of Recent Decisions.
S.L.T. (Sh.Ct.)	Scots Law Times Sheriff Court reports.
S.P.L.P.	Scottish Planning Law and Practice.
T.L.R.	Times Law Reports.
W.L.R.	Weekly Law Reports.

CHAPTER 1

INTRODUCTION

MANY would regard the title of this book as something of a contradiction in terms. Planning by agreement would seem to be a consummation devoutly to be wished for but rarely achieved. However, planning by agreement, as one commentator has observed, "is not a manifestation of the ultimate in democracy within our planning system."[1] Indeed, the practice has been criticised as striking in some instances "at the foundation of the system of planning control itself."[2] Yet it has some powerful advocates. In particular, the Sheaf Committee in their report in 1972[3] considered that agreements between local planning authorities and developers had a useful role to play in securing the release of adequate land to acccommodate the demand for housing in the south-east of England. As Hoyes points out "agreements enable planning permission to be granted where otherwise it would be refused and the proposed development delayed because there is a significant planning objection to immediate development."[4] He goes on to suggest that "[i]f the development control system is to function effectively in the immediate future, particularly in the sense of the management of change, agreements will need to be more widely used, so as to avoid a significant further slowing down of development."

Planning by agreement, however, suggests a process of bargaining and much of the controversy over the practice has centred on the uneasy relationship between the private bargaining process on the one hand and the public licensing of development on the other. The latter operates within well-established parameters; the former appears to operate free from obvious restraint.[5] Yet as Grant

---

[1] T. Hoyes, "Conditions and Agreements—the Developer's Viewpoint" in *Development Control—Thirty Years On* (Journal of Planning and Environment Law Occasional Paper, Sweet and Maxwell, 1979).
[2] "Planning Gain," *Report by the Property Advisory Group* (HMSO, 1981), para. 6.07.
[3] *Report of Working Party on Local Authority/Private Enterprise Partnership Schemes*, Department of the Environment (HMSO, 1972).
[4] T. Hoyes, *supra*.
[5] But see now the advice in SDD Circular 22/1984.

observes, "[p]lanning agreements are as old as public land use planning itself."[6] And the power to negotiate agreements is clear beyond doubt. The power to enter into planning agreements was first included in the Housing, Town Planning etc. Act 1909. Similar provision was subsequently incorporated into the Town and Country Planning (Scotland) Act 1932. Section 33 of that Act provided that where any person was willing to agree that his land should be made subject to conditions "restricting the planning, development or use thereof," a local authority might enter into an agreement with him to that effect. It seems that this provision was mainly intended to assist planning authorities in keeping land free of development without their becoming liable to pay compensation. The 1932 Act did not, however, permit authorities to give any commitment as to how they would use their planning powers in the future. In *Ransom & Luck* v. *Surbiton Borough Council*[7] it was held that the sole purpose of the corresponding provision of the English legislation was to allow local authorities to accept undertakings from land-owners and to enable authorities to enforce such undertakings. It did not permit a local authority to contract not to use its statutory powers or to use those powers in a particular way.

The power to enter into agreements was widened in several respects by the Town and Country Planning (Scotland) Act 1947. Not only could an authority enter into agreements for the purpose of restricting the development or use of land, an agreement could also *regulate* the development or use of land. An agreement might also contain incidental and consequential provisions, including provisions of a financial character. More importantly, the legislation provided (albeit in a strangely negative fashion) that planning authorities could, within certain limits, give valid commitments in an agreement as to how they would exercise their statutory powers in the future.[8]

Until the coming into operation of the Town and Country Planning (Scotland) Act 1969 each agreement made under the provisions of the 1947 Act required the approval of the Secretary of State for Scotland. There seems little doubt that this requirement had an inhibiting effect upon the use of agreements. It has been stated that between 1947 and the coming into operation of the 1969 Act, only six agreements were made in Scotland.[9] The need

---

[6] M. Grant, *Urban Planning Law* (Sweet and Maxwell, 1982, 1st Supplement, 1986), p. 362.
[7] [1949] Ch. 180; see Chap. 6.
[8] See Chap. 6.
[9] Isabel Bruce, "Section 50 Agreements and Enforcement" (thesis submitted for Diploma in Town Planning, University of Strathclyde, 1979).

for ministerial approval was abolished by the 1969 Act. The power to enter into agreements was continued in section 50 of the Town and Country Planning (Scotland) Act 1972 ("the 1972 Act"). Section 50(1) of the 1972 Act provides:

> "A planning authority may enter into an agreement with any person interested in land in their area (in so far as the interest of that person enables him to bind the land) for the purpose of restricting or regulating the development or use of the land, either permanently or during such period as may be prescribed by the agreement."[10]

What then is the purpose of this specific power in section 50 to negotiate planning agreements? Unlike individuals, who are entitled to do anything not prohibited by the law, local authorities, as creatures of statute, are only entitled to act within the limits of the powers conferred upon them by Parliament. The importance of this doctrine—the *ultra vires* doctrine—is that if a local authority act without statutory warrant, that action may be declared invalid. Local authorities have, however, always possessed the power to take any action which can reasonably be regarded as incidental to the discharge of their statutory functions,[11] a power which has been put on a statutory basis by section 69 of the Local Government (Scotland) Act 1973.[12]

Local authorities do not, therefore, need specific powers to make contracts. If a planning authority, for the better discharge of their planning functions, wish to enter into an agreement with another party there is nothing to prevent them from so doing.[13] Any such agreement would be enforceable in the courts in the normal fashion by the parties to it. However, in the absence of specific statutory authority (such as is provided by section 50[14]), obligations contained in any such contract, even though related to land, will only be enforceable against the individual with whom the agreement was made; they will not (unless contained in a feu writ or a disposition) "run with the land," *i.e.* they will not be

---

[10] For convenience a copy of s.50 is reproduced in App. 1.

[11] See *Attorney-General* v. *Great Eastern Ry Co.* (1880) 5 App.Cas. 473, *per* Lord Chancellor Selborne. See also *D. & J. Nicol* v. *Dundee Harbour Trs.*, 1915 S.C.(H.L.) 7; *Graham* v. *Glasgow Corporation*, 1936 S.C. 108; *Glasgow Corporation* v. *Flint*, 1966 S.C. 108.

[12] That section provides that a local authority "shall have power to do anything . . . which is calculated to facilitate, or is conducive or incidental to, the discharge of any of their functions."

[13] See, *e.g. Jones* v. *Secretary of State for Wales* (1974) 72 L.G.R. 583.

[14] Section 50 is not unique. There are other statutory powers which provide for the making of agreements which run with the land. Some of these provisions are considered in Chap. 9.

binding upon future owners of the land.[15] In the case of an agreement entered into for planning purposes, this would often be a considerable drawback from the planning authority's point of view.

The great practical advantage that section 50 offers to planning authorities is that if the agreement is recorded in the Register of Sasines,[16] it is enforceable against the owner of the land for the time being.[17] In effect, the agreement is binding upon the land and is enforceable not just against the individual with whom it was made but also against his successors in title.

The value of this aspect of section 50 may perhaps be illustrated by an example. A planning authority may consider that on road safety grounds it would be inappropriate to approve an application for permission to develop a site as a new shopping complex until improvements to the public road network have been carried out. The local roads authority may not be in a position to give priority to such works. The developer, realising that these road works are the key to his getting planning permission, may be prepared to carry them out himself. However, it appears to be the law that

---

[15] See *Campbell's Trs.* v. *Glasgow Corporation* (1902) 4 F. 752. Under an agreement with Glasgow Corporation, several landowners undertook not to build upon a strip of land, the Corporation to be entitled at any time to utilise the strip of land for road purposes. The agreement was recorded in the Register of Sasines. The First Division of the Court of Session held that in spite of its having been recorded, the agreement was merely a personal contract; the undertaking was therefore not binding upon a party who had acquired the strip of land from the original contracting parties. In the course of his judgment (in which the other members of the First Division concurred) Lord Kinnear said:

"The agreement is no doubt an onerous deed, and it is not disputed that as a matter of fact it has been recorded in the Register of Sasines. But the term 'duly recorded' which is used by the parties, seems to me singularly inappropriate, inasmuch as it has no claim to a place on the register, since it is a merely personal contract, containing no conveyance of the land and no feudal clauses of any kind."

[16] Where registration of title is in operation, the registration of a s.50 agreement in the Land Register will have the same effect as recording in the Sasine Register—see Land Registration (Scotland) Act 1979, s.29(2).

[17] Subsection (2) of s.50 provides that:

"An agreement made under this section with any person interested in land, may, if the agreement shall have been recorded in the appropriate Register of Sasines, be enforceable at the instance of the planning authority against persons deriving title to the land from the person with whom the agreement was entered into:

Provided that no such agreement shall at any time be enforceable against a third party who shall have in bona fide onerously acquired right (whether completed by infeftment or not) to the land prior to the agreement being recorded as aforesaid or against any person deriving title from such third party."

the planning authority could not grant permission subject to a condition that the developer carry out the necessary road works[18]; so far as their ordinary development control powers are concerned, the planning authority must either refuse the application as premature or grant planning permission and rely on the goodwill of the developer to carry out the road improvements. Even if the developer gave an undertaking of some kind that he would carry out the necessary works, that undertaking, although it might be enforceable against the developer,[19] would not run with the land unless it were incorporated in a recorded section 50 agreement; if the undertaking were not contained in such an agreement there would be nothing to prevent the developer, in spite of his undertaking, disposing of the land to some third party with the benefit of the permission but free from any obligation to carry out the works. If, however, the developer and the planning authority entered into an agreement under section 50 and that agreement were recorded in the Register of Sasines, the terms of the agreement would be binding upon successors in title to the land. The authority's position is safeguarded by the recorded agreement and they could grant planning permission secure in the knowledge that the improvements to the highway would be carried out as part of the scheme of development.

There is a real possibility that an agreement made for the purpose of restricting or regulating the development or use of land might fall foul of the principle that a public authority must not enter into any commitment which is incompatible with the proper exercise of their statutory powers in the future—in effect, the authority must not so tie their hands in advance that they disable themselves from carrying out their statutory responsibilities. In its operation this principle can be somewhat uncertain but an agreement under which an authority undertook to grant planning permission or to refrain from taking enforcement action or in some other way to fetter the future exercise of their development control powers might run the risk of being held *ultra vires*. However, it seems clear that section 50, though it does so by implication rather than directly, enables a planning authority, in some circumstances to enter into agreements which have the effect of fettering their

---

[18] See, *e.g. Hall & Co.* v. *Shoreham-by-sea UDC* [1964] 1 W.L.R. 240. But see *Grampian Regional Council* v. *City of Aberdeen District Council*, 1984 S.L.T. 197.

[19] *E.g.* under s.40 of the Roads (Scotland) Act 1984. See also *Augier* v. *Secretary of State for the Environment* (1978) 38 P. & C.R. 219 (*sub. nom. Hildenborough Village Preservation Association* v. *Secretary of State for the Environment* [1978] J.P.L. 708), discussed in Chap. 7.

statutory powers. The law on this matter is very complex and is considered in more detail below.[20] We would suggest, however, that it is at least clear that it is a further purpose of section 50 to confer upon planning authorities somewhat wider contractual powers than are normally possessed by public authorities.

Against this background, the object of this book is, first of all, to examine the law relating to the use of such agreements and to indicate what legal restraints there are upon the practice of planning by agreement. While we would not wish to over-emphasise the legal problems, important and difficult questions can arise as to the precise scope of section 50. Some of these we have touched on briefly above. They include the application of general administrative law principles to the exercise of contractual powers by planning authorities, the relationship between general development control powers and the powers conferred by section 50, and the relationship between statutory planning powers and the common law of contract. So far as we are aware, there has been no litigation in the Scottish courts on the powers conferred by section 50 of the 1972 Act and there has been surprisingly little judicial scrutiny of the corresponding provision in section 52 of the (English) Town and Country Planning Act 1971. That being so, our discussion at some points in the book is inevitably of a somewhat speculative nature.

Our second objective in this book is to describe the purposes for which agreements are being employed. Research carried out by two students in 1978 indicated an increasing use in Scotland of agreements made under section 50 of the 1972 Act.[21] Unfortunately, the results were not published. In England research carried out by Professor Jeffrey Jowell[22] and Dr J. N. Hawke[23] showed a widespread use of agreements made under section 52 of the Town and Country Planning Act 1971 and much has been written on English law and practice on the subject.[24] There are, however, important differences in the effects of section 50 of the 1972 Act and its English counterpart. To establish the position in Scotland

---

[20] See Chap. 6.

[21] J. Douglas Cramond, "Planning by Agreement" (thesis submitted for degree of B.Sc., Heriot-Watt University 1979); Isabel Bruce, "Section 50 Agreements and Enforcement" (thesis submitted for Diploma in Town Planning, University of Strathclyde, 1979).

[22] See "Bargaining in Development Control" [1977] J.P.L. 414.

[23] See "Planning Agreements in Practice" [1981] J.P.L. 5 and 86.

[24] A fairly full bibliography is included in App. 3.

we conducted two surveys, the first in 1982[25] and the second in 1987. The results are discussed in some detail in Chapter 8 but it is apparent that the use that is being made of planning agreements has increased greatly in the last few years. The response to our surveys shows that since the reorganisation of local government in 1975, at least 661 agreements have been completed and we believe the actual number completed may be considerably in excess of this figure.

Planning authorities are empowered to enter into agreements "for the purpose of restricting or regulating the development or use" of land. These are wide words and the range of purposes for which agreements can be used is very wide. In practice, however, it is clear that the purposes of almost all agreements entered into in Scotland under section 50 relate in some way to the development control functions of planning authorities and that, in the great majority of cases, planning agreements are triggered by the making of an application for planning permission.

Planning agreements have in many cases been used as a means of reinforcing development control powers. In particular, they may be used in order to impose restrictions which it would be difficult or impossible to enforce by means of a condition attached to a grant of planning permission. In other cases agreements have been used to overcome certain of the limitations which the law imposes upon the use of conditions or to provide means of avoiding the doubts which can easily exist as to the precise scope of those limitations. There are other ways too in which agreements may enable planning authorities to exert more detailed or more continuous control over the development or use of land than is possible with ordinary development control powers, and to provide a more flexible and more positive means of achieving planning objectives. In particular, a planning authority may well feel that an agreement is likely to prove a more effective means of control than their ordinary development control powers, in that an agreement can be enforced in the ordinary way in the courts, thus avoiding the need for enforcement action under the provisions of Part V of the 1972 Act, a process which can prove time-consuming and cannot be guaranteed to succeed. In effect, a planning authority can, through an agreement, exert the sort of control over land use

---

[25] See J. Rowan-Robinson and E. Young, *Planning by Agreement: The Law and Practice* (Scottish Planning Law and Practice Occasional Paper No. 4, The Planning Exchange, 1982). See also, J. Rowan-Robinson and M. G. Lloyd, *Land Development and the Infrastructure Lottery* (T. & T. Clark Ltd., 1988), Chap. 4.

which they would otherwise only be able to exert if they owned the land in question.

Agreements can, for example, provide a means of regulating the use of land outwith the control of the developer; an agreement can be used to impose restrictions on the alienation of land; and sometimes they have been used to transfer the cost of the necessary roads or sewers or whatever to the developer and thus permit development to proceed immediately.

From what we have said, and from our more detailed discussion in Chapter 8, it would seem that the bargaining process provides a useful supplement to normal development control powers. Obligations in agreements are directed towards the removal of difficulties arising from the development proposed. It would seem that, to a large extent, the purpose of an agreement, as Walton J. observed in *Western Fish Products Ltd.* v. *Penwith District Council*,[26] is to "enable the local planning authority to control matters which it might otherwise have no power to control by the imposition of conditions on any planning permission."

However, there are indications that in some cases, planning authorities, sometimes at the invitation of developers, have been going somewhat beyond the simple removal of obstacles arising from the proposed development and have been securing from developers benefits for the community which are unrelated, or not directly related, to the proposed development. This is a practice which has been pursued rather more extensively in England than in Scotland and, perhaps not surprisingly, has provoked very considerable controversy. Some of the arguments that have been advanced for and against the pursuit of what is generally referred to as "planning gain" are rehearsed in Chapter 10. The definitions of "planning gain" vary but for present purposes we may define it as some benefit to the community that is of no commercial advantage to the developer who provides the benefit. It is, in effect, the price he pays for receiving planning permission for profitable development.

There is, of course, no way in which a landowner can be compelled to enter into a section 50 agreement. Why should a landowner agree to be a party to an agreement? It is clear in many cases that it is quite simply because a developer hopes to obtain a favourable decision of some kind from the planning authority— for example, on an application for planning permission or an application for listed building consent—and anticipates or realises that he stands a much better chance of being allowed to implement

---

[26] Unreported, November 19, 1977.

his proposals if he is prepared to enter into an agreement containing provisions which render the proposals more acceptable to the planning authority. The developer's willingness to enter into an agreement may, in effect, make the difference between grant and refusal of permission. The developer may well consider it more advantageous to enter into an agreement with the planning authority than face the uncertain prospect of an appeal to the Secretary of State and the certain delay and expense that such an appeal will entail.

Although section 50 agreements clearly play an important role in controlling and guiding land use change it should be noted that there are a number of other statutory powers which provide for the making of agreements governing the use, development or management of land. Mention has already been made of the general power in section 69 of the Local Government (Scotland) Act 1973 to do anything that can reasonably be regarded as incidental to the discharge of authorities' statutory functions. Other more specific powers exist under the Sewerage (Scotland) Act 1968 and the Roads (Scotland) Act 1984 which may in some instances offer an alternative to section 50. And in rural areas, where the jurisdiction of planning authorities is limited, the bargaining process is the principal mechanism for controlling and guiding land use change in the public interest. A far greater part of the land area of Scotland is governed by statutory agreements negotiated by the Nature Conservancy Council, the Department of Agriculture and Fisheries for Scotland and the National Trust for Scotland than is subject to section 50 agreements. These and other agreements are discussed in more detail in Chapter 9. However, our principal concern in this book is with section 50 agreements and it is to the detail of section 50 that we now turn.

CHAPTER 2

THE PARTIES TO A SECTION 50 AGREEMENT

SECTION 50 begins: "(1) A planning authority may enter into an agreement with any person interested in land in their area (in so far as the interest of that person enables him to bind the land)." In this chapter we consider aspects of the law relating to the parties to a section 50 agreement.

Planning authority

In the rural regions and island areas of Scotland, *i.e.* in the Highlands, Borders, and Dumfries and Galloway regions, in the Western Isles, Orkney and Shetland—all planning functions are discharged by the regional and islands councils as general planning authorities. In the rest of the country planning functions are divided between regional and district councils.[1] Section 50 refers to a "planning authority" entering into an agreement. The Local Government (Scotland) Act 1973 provides that wherever the term "planning authority" appears in any statute, it is, unless otherwise provided, to be construed as a reference to a general planning authority or to a district planning authority.[2] It seems clear, therefore, that as originally enacted section 50 only empowered general and district planning authorities to make agreements. It did not empower regional planning authorities to enter into agreements.

It is certainly the case that so far as "pure" town planning matters are concerned the role of the region is essentially a strategic one,[3] but these strategic functions and the regions' responsibilities for the provision of important services with land use implications— roads, water, sewerage and education—may well result in a regional planning authority having a substantial interest in the impact of an individual planning application. Furthermore, a regional planning authority can in certain circumstances direct that

---

[1] See Local Government (Scotland) Act 1973, s.172 and Sched. 22.
[2] S.172(3).
[3] Regional planning functions are those described as such in Pt. I of Sched. 22 to the Local Government (Scotland) Act 1973, together with the functions conferred on regional or general planning authorities by Pt. IX of that Act.

10

an application for planning permission should be referred to them instead of being dealt with by the district planning authority.[4] The sort of major development proposal which is likely to be the subject of "call in" by the region may well raise issues which it might be appropriate to regulate by way of a section 50 agreement. The omission was remedied by the Local Government and Planning (Scotland) Act 1982[5] which added to section 50 a new subsection (4) which provides that the term "planning authority" is, for the purposes of section 50, to include a regional planning authority (see Appendix 1).

The three regional planning authorities that responded to our questionnaire indicated that they have since made use of the power to negotiate section 50 agreements, one of them extensively. These agreements have been employed, for the most part, to sort out servicing arrangements in connection with major developments, particularly major retailing and housing schemes.

Alex Samuels has suggested[6] that it would be competent for the Secretary of State to enter into an agreement under section 52 of the (English) Town and Country Planning Act 1971. He states: "if it be the case that on appeal the Secretary of State can do all that the local planning authority could do, then presumably it must follow that he can, if the developer is willing, enter directly into such an agreement, which would be binding upon the local planning authority." It seems to us that this overstates the power of the Secretary of State. On appeal he is entitled to deal with the application in question as if it had been made to him in the first place.[7] We do not think that this power is wide enough to include the power to enter into an agreement under section 50 of the 1972 Act.

Where an application for planning permission is "called in" by the Secretary of State, section 50 is not among the powers stated to be applicable in connection with the determination by the minister of the application.[8] Nor is the power to enter into agreements included among the default powers of the Secretary of State.[9]

"Any person interested in land"
The planning authority may enter into an agreement under

---

[4] See Local Government (Scotland) Act 1973, s.179 as substituted by the Local Government and Planning (Scotland) Act 1982, s.69(2) and Sched. 3, para. 24.
[5] See Sched. 2, para. 14.
[6] "Planning Agreements: Their Use and Misuse" (1978) 142 L.G.R. 609.
[7] 1972 Act, s.33(3).
[8] See 1972 Act, s.32.
[9] See 1972 Act, s.260.

section 50 with "any person interested in land in their area (in so far as the interest of that person enables him to bind the land)."

The phrase "any person interested in land" has given rise to very considerable difficulty in practice. It is, in the words of Eveleigh L.J., a phrase of "widely differing capabilities."[10] For example, an applicant for planning permission is commonly a purchaser of the subject land under conditional missives. In common parlance he may be said to be a person "interested in the land". Is he a person with whom a planning authority may enter into a section 50 agreement? In *Jones* v. *Secretary of State for Wales*[11] Lord Denning expressed the view that the corresponding wording in section 52 of the (English) Town and Country Planning Act 1971 (which is similar but not identical—see below) did not encompass a person who is interested in the development of land but has not yet acquired title to it. That case arose out of an agreement which provided that a planned redevelopment should be carried out by means of a partnership scheme. The local planning authority were to draw up the plans for the development and to assemble the necessary land, while the other party to the agreement, a development company, was to provide expertise and a large part of the finance for the development. The validity of the partnership scheme was called in question in the courts. The agreement did not, it seems, refer specifically to the statutory powers under which it was made. At one stage in the proceedings it was apparently suggested by the planning authority that the partnership scheme was authorised by section 52 of the Town and Country Planning Act 1971. The Court of Appeal took the view that it was not so authorised. Section 52 only applied to an agreement with a person who was, in Lord Denning's words, "*already* interested in the land," whereas, he said, "the burden of the arrangement here was as to a developer who was not already interested in the land but was proposing to develop it." The court considered, however, that the partnership agreement was probably within the local authority's powers under other statutory provisions.

SDD Circular 22/1984 adopts what has been described as a "very narrow construction"[12] of the word "interest":

> "Only a person whose interest at the time of signing the agreement enables him to bind the land may enter into a Section 50 agreement, namely, the person whose name appears on the Register as the owner

[10] *Pennine Raceway Ltd.* v. *Kirklees Metropolitan Borough Council* [1983] Q.B. 382.
[11] (1974) 28 P. & C.R. 280; 72 L.G.R. 583.
[12] P. Gannon, "Section 50 agreements" (1985) 15 S.P.L.P. 56.

or the lessee under a recorded lease. A person whose only interest is
that of developer or prospective purchaser may not enter into such
agreements."[13]

The circular does not go on to explain why it adopts this narrow
construction but it is presumably influenced by the words "in so
far as the interest of that person enables him to bind the land"
which appear in brackets in subsection (1) of section 50 and which
have no counterpart in section 52 of the English Act; and also by
subsection (2) of section 50 which provides that an agreement
made under the section with any person interested in land may, if
it has been recorded, be enforceable at the instance of the planning
authority against singular successors. Only a person whose name
appears on the Register as the owner or the lessee under a recorded
lease may bind the land in this way. The narrow construction
supports the view that the principal function of section 50 is
not so much to confer new contractual powers upon planning
authorities—adequate powers already exist,[14] but rather to give
planning authorities the right in prescribed circumstances to
enforce agreements against singular successors. It necessitates
reading "any person interested in land" not simply as "any person
having an interest in land" but as "any person having a recordable
interest in land."

It has been argued that this reads too much into the provision
and that it should be given a broader construction[15] which would
encompass, for example, uninfeft proprietors and all those with
an occupational interest in the land such as lessees under a lease
of no more than 20 years duration and licensees. At first sight the
dictum of Eveleigh L.J. in the English Court of Appeal in *Pennine
Raceway Ltd.* v. *Kirklees Metropolitan Borough Council*[16] would
seem to support a broader construction. The case turned on the
question whether the plaintiffs were persons "interested in land"
within the meaning of section 164 of the Town and Country
Planning Act 1971 for the purposes of a claim for compensation
following the revocation of a planning permission. The plaintiffs
had been granted what appeared to be a licence by the owner to
use land for motor racing within the scope of the planning
permission. They had subsequently incurred some expense in
erecting barriers and fences and laying tarmac which was rendered
abortive by the revocation of the permission. As a result of the

---

[13] Para. 8.
[14] See, generally Chap. 1.
[15] See, *e.g.* P. Gannon, "Section 50 Agreements" (1985) 15 S.P.L.P. 56.
[16] [1983] Q.B. 382.

revocation they were also now liable to restore the land to its condition before the work started. Their claim for compensation under section 164 was rejected by the Lands Tribunal on the ground that they were not persons "interested in the land". The Court of Appeal, however, considered they had sufficient interest and allowed the claim. Eveleigh L.J., whose attention was drawn to the similar wording in section 52(1) of the 1971 Act which enables a local planning authority to enter into an agreement with any person interested in land and to the possible limitation imposed on it by subsection (2) which, like section 50(2) of the Scottish Act, provides for enforcement of agreements against successors in title, observed "I cannot read subsection (2) as limiting the meaning of subsection (1) so as to make subsection (1) apply only to persons who have an interest in land in a strict conveyancing sense. We are dealing with a statute which controls use and operations on land and provides compensation. It is not a conveyancing statute." The effect of subsection (2), which enables an agreement to be enforced against successors in title, was simply, he said, that if a person had such an interest which was transferable and had transferred it, then the agreement may be enforced against the transferee.

The comment on the general effect of section 52(2) of the English Act would seem equally applicable to section 50(2) of the Scottish Act. Recording an agreement in the Register of Sasines or in the Land Register for Scotland is not compulsory and it is questionable, therefore, whether subsection (2) should be read as limiting the meaning of "any person interested in land" in subsection (1). However, it is difficult to escape the conclusion that the words "in so far as the interest of that person enables him to bind the land," which appear in brackets in subsection (1) and which do not appear in the English Act, intend interests to be construed in a strict conveyancing sense. The point, however, remains unsettled.

If the narrow construction advanced in SDD Circular 22/1984 is adopted, planning authorities will, nonetheless, have to bear in mind that an individual can, of course, only bind his own interest and there may be several separate interests existing in the same parcel of land at any one time. A landlord cannot, for example, burden a tenant's interest (unless there is some provision to that effect in the lease); and an owner may not be in a position to burden land without the consent of a heritable creditor.[17] Planning

---

[17] See D. W. Cockburn, "Section 50 Agreements: Some Aspects for the Conveyancer" (1984) 12 S.P.L.P. 38.

authorities will have to investigate title (in practice they do) and they will have to consider whether, in order to ensure that the agreement is effective, other parties with different interests in the land, for example, the proprietor of a servitude right, need to be joined or at least consent to it. If an obligation affecting land is to be effective in the short term as well as in the longer term, then it may be that *all* persons who currently have some interest in the land should be joined as parties to the agreement, including those with interests which are incapable of binding the land such as lessees under unrecorded leases. If the latter were omitted, they might be able to ignore the agreement for as long as their interest subsists.[18] To avoid uncertainty about whether they may properly be parties to the agreement under section 50, planning authorities may employ their other contractual powers[19] and, if considered appropriate, these may be recited in the agreement along with section 50.

Although it would seem from what we have said above that section 50 only authorises the making of an agreement with a person who has already acquired an appropriate interest in the land, it is clear that the planning authority could under their other powers,[20] make a valid contract with, for example, a prospective developer who does not yet possess such an interest. Such an agreement would not, of course, be binding upon the land.

A "bona fide" purchaser

Subsection (2) of section 50 provides that:

> "no such agreement shall at any time be enforceable against a third party who shall have in bona fide onerously acquired right (whether completed by infeftment or not) to the land prior to the agreement being recorded as aforesaid or against any persons deriving title from such third party."

The meaning of the words "bona fide" as used in this provision could be very important in a case where a landowner who had entered into a section 50 agreement proposed to dispose of the land before the agreement had been recorded. Would a purchaser acquiring land for value[21] be free from the obligations contained

---

[18] *Ibid.*

[19] See, generally Chap. 1.

[20] *Ibid.* See also, *Augier* v. *Secretary of State for the Environment* (1978) 38 P. & C.R. 219 (reported *sub. nom. Hildenborough Village Preservation Association* v. *Secretary of State for the Environment* [1978] J.P.L. 708).

[21] Presumably this is all that is meant by "onerously."

in the agreement? Subsection (2) of section 50 has not been
subjected to judicial scrutiny but we would tentatively suggest that
the answer to that question will simply depend on whether or not
the purchaser had knowledge of the existence of the agreement.
We think that some support for this view can be derived from
Stodart v. *Dalzell*[22] and *Rodger (Builders) Ltd.* v. *Fawdry*.[23]

In *Stodart* Lord Gifford accepted that it was an important
principle of the law "that a singular successor is entitled to be free
from the personal obligations of his predecessor, and to take the
subject unaffected by any burden not appearing on the title or the
records." "But", he went on to say, "the singular successor has
only this right if he was in ignorance of any obligations or deeds
granted by the seller relative to the subject, and if he was in all
respects a bona fide purchaser, without notice of any right in any
third party or of any circumstances imposing a duty of inquiry."[24]
In *Rodger (Builders) Ltd.* it was held that where an intending
purchaser of heritable property was aware of an earlier contract
for the sale of the property, his failure to make inquiry about that
prior contract was sufficient *per se* to deprive him of the character
of a bona fide purchaser.

We would therefore suggest that if, for example, the planning
permission to which a section 50 agreement was linked made
reference to the agreement, then it would be difficult for a
purchaser who had seen the permission to argue that he had
acquired right to the land in bona fide and was therefore not
bound by the agreement.

Several planning authorities have sought to avoid potential
problems of this kind by incorporating in their section 50 agreements a provision prohibiting any disposal of the land until the
agreement has been recorded.

[22] (1876) 4 R. 236 (distinguished in *Wallace* v. *Simmers*, 1960 S.C. 255).
[23] 1950 S.C. 483.
[24] The law may not be as broad as this dictum might suggest. In *Wallace* (*supra*)
the Lord President (Clyde) stated that Lord Gifford's opinion in *Stodart* had to
be read in the light of the circumstances in that case.

CHAPTER 3

"RESTRICTING OR REGULATING" DEVELOPMENT

SUBSECTION (1) of section 50 provides that a planning authority may enter into an agreement with any person interested in land:

> "for the purpose of restricting or regulating the development or use of the land . . . and any such agreement may contain such incidental and consequential provisions (including provisions of a financial character) as appear to the planning authority to be necessary or expedient for the purposes of the agreement."

The phrase "for the purpose of restricting or regulating the development or use of land" appears to impose some limit upon the scope of agreements. It seems to us, however, that the limits are difficult to define with any precision. While the words "restricting or regulating" clearly permit the inclusion in a section 50 agreement of negative obligations—for example, provisions placing restrictions upon the use of premises—the extent to which an agreement can impose obligations of a positive nature— obligations requiring, for example, the provision of infrastructure or the allocation of land for some public purpose—is far from clear. It is this uncertainty which we are addressing in this chapter. It should be emphasised at this stage that questions about the propriety of imposing particular obligations in an agreement linked to a planning application (and our research shows that almost all agreements are linked in this way) are left over for consideration in Chapter 5.

There has been a good deal of discussion in the academic and professional texts and journals of the question of *enforceability* of positive obligations contained in agreements made under section 52 of the Town and Country Planning Act 1971.[1] Much of that discussion is not directly relevant to Scotland and this is not the place for lengthy consideration of peculiarly English problems.

---

[1] See, in particular J. F. Garner, "Agreements Under Section 25" [1949] J.P.L. 628; Malcolm Grant, "Planning by Agreement" [1975] J.P.L. 501; Michael Aves, "Enforcing Section 52 Agreements" [1976] J.P.L. 216; John Alder, *Development Control*, pp. 129–132; L. R. Tucker, "Planning Agreements—The Twilight Zone of Ultra Vires" [1978] J.P.L. 806; and Martin Loughlin, "Planning Gain: Law, Policy and Practice" (1981) 1 Oxford Jo. of Legal Studies 61.

Subsection (1) of the 1971 Act is, however, almost identical in its terms to subsection (1) of section 50 of the 1972 Act and it seems reasonable to assume that Parliament must have intended the scope of the powers to enter into agreements to be broadly similar on both sides of the border. The debate about the English legislation and the common law background against which it operates may therefore have some relevance in Scotland as perhaps throwing a little light on the meaning to be given to the words "restricting or regulating". It therefore seems appropriate to give a brief account of the setting in which section 52 of the 1971 Act operates south of the border and the conclusions which some English writers have been led to draw as to the scope of the provision.

Digression: positive covenants in English law

Under the general law of England, positive covenants relating to land can bind the person who originally undertakes the obligation but can never bind his successors in title. Negative or restrictive covenants will be binding upon successors in title provided that the covenants conform to the strict requirements which were spelt out in *Tulk* v. *Moxhay*.[2] In particular, covenants must be taken for the benefit of adjacent land and the person seeking to enforce the covenant must be in possession of that land.[3] While a specific statutory provision may override the common law and provide, for example, that positive covenants may run with the land, clear words are required for this. Section 126 of the Housing Act 1974, which is mentioned below, provided an example of such clear wording. A comparison of the wording of subsection (2) of section 52 of the 1971 Act[4] with the judgment in *Tulk* v. *Moxhay* suggests that the subsection should simply be seen as machinery designed to confer upon the local planning authority the standing of an

---

[2] (1848) 2 Ph. 774.

[3] The requirements laid down in *Tulk* v. *Moxhay* are:
   (i) The covenant must be negative in character;
   (ii) The burden of the covenant must have been intended to run with the land;
   (iii) The covenant must have been made for the benefit of adjoining land held by the covenantee at the time of the covenant;
   (iv) If the plaintiff is not the original covenantee, he must show that the benefit of the covenant has passed to him.

[4] Subsection (2) of section 52 is in the following terms:
   "An agreement made under this section with any person interested in land may be enforced by the local planning authority against persons deriving title under that person in respect of that land, as if the local planning authority were possessed of adjacent land and as if the agreement had been expressed to be made for the benefit of that land."

adjacent landowner and so to enable the authority to enforce the covenant where they would have no standing to do so at common law.[5]

> "Parliament was minded to make use of that very valuable principle [*i.e.* the principle established in *Tulk* v. *Moxhay*] but, in order to do so it had to put the local authority artificially into the same position as a neighbouring landowner, because a restrictive covenant entered into by the landowner with the local authority would not bind the land under the ordinary law, for it would not be made for the benefit of adjoining land."[6]

In other words, it is by no means clear that section 52 was intended to enlarge on the common law position; rather it appears to have been designed to allow local planning authorities to take advantage of the common law principle through the medium of an agreement. It would seem, therefore, that in England an agreement under section 52 could not include a positive covenant which would be binding upon successors in title.[7] In order to overcome the problems to which this could give rise, especially in connection with major redevelopment schemes, in the 1960s and early 1970s a number of English local authorities obtained additional powers through Private Acts.[8] These private enactments provided for the inclusion in agreements of positive covenants enforceable against successors in title.

A general solution to the difficulty was provided by the Housing Act 1974. Giving effect to a recommendation of the Sheaf Committee,[9] section 126 of that Act provided that agreements made under other statutory provisions (including section 52 of the 1971 Act) could contain positive covenants which could be enforceable against successors in title. That provision has now been replaced by section 33 of the Local Government (Miscellaneous Provisions) Act 1982.[10]

---

[5] See the comments of Lord Denning M.R. in *Gee* v. *The National Trust* (1966) 17 P. & C.R. 7 (dealing with the similarly-worded provision in the National Trust Act 1937).

[6] *Ransom & Luck* v. *Surbiton Borough Council* [1949] Ch. 180, *per* Lord Greene M.R. at p. 194.

[7] For a contrary view on this see Michael Aves, "Enforcing Section 52 Agreements" [1976] J.P.L. 216.

[8] See Malcolm Grant, "Planning by Agreement" [1975] J.P.L. 501.

[9] *Working Party on Local Authority/Private Enterprise Partnership Schemes* para. 52.

[10] Section 33(2) of the Local Government (Miscellaneous Provisions) Act 1982 provides:

> "If, in a case where this section applies—
> (a) the instrument contains a covenant on the part of any person having an

Positive obligations

While there has been much discussion of the question of the enforceability of positive covenants contained in agreements under section 52,[11] there has been much less discussion of the question (much more relevant in Scotland) whether, leaving aside matters of enforceability and the common law background, the terms of the section are wide enough to permit the statutory powers to be employed for the purpose of pursuing positive, as well as restrictive, objectives. The section states that an agreement can be entered into for the purpose of "restricting or regulating" the development or use of land and there can therefore be doubts about the validity of an agreement which seeks to impose positive obligations upon a developer.

Some English writers take the view that the words of section 52 cannot be interpreted in isolation from the common law background; the section has to be read, it is said, with reference to the conceptual framework of restrictive covenants. For those writers the form of section 52 (and of subsection (2) in particular) is, in Loughlin's words, "indicative not only of the method of enforcement but also of the nature of the provision itself." This approach can, at its extreme, lead to the conclusion that: "To use a section 52 agreement to impose a positive requirement would be outside the ambit of the power conferred on the local authority."[12]

Loughlin[13] argues against this "formalistic" approach to the legislation, saying that those who adopt this approach pay inadequate regard to the purpose of section 52. He argues that a "purposive" approach to the legislation should be adopted. (The "purposive" approach to statutory interpretation which is followed

---

     interest in land, being a covenant to carry out any works or do any other thing on or in relation to that land, and

  (b) the instrument defines the land to which the covenant relates, being land in which that person has an interest at the time the instrument is executed, and

  (c) the covenant is expressed to be one to which this section or section 126 of the Housing Act 1974 (which is superseded by this section) applies,

the covenant shall be enforceable (without any limit of time) against any person deriving title from the original covenantor in respect of his interest in any of the land defined as mentioned in paragraph (b) above and any person deriving title under him in respect of any lesser interest in that land as if that person had also been an original covenanting party in respect of the interest for the time being held by him."

[11] See, in particular the articles cited in n. 1 *supra*.

[12] L. R. Tucker, "Planning Agreements—The Twilight Zone of Ultra Vires" [1978] J.P.L. 806.

[13] See the article cited in n. 1 *supra*, pp. 78–82.

by some, but by no means all, judges[14] stresses the importance of seeking to promote the "general legislative purpose" or policy underlying the particular provision. This approach is often contrasted with the stricter "literal" approach in which great weight is laid upon the need for close and careful scrutiny of the actual words used by the legislature).[15] Taking a purposive approach to section 52 would, in Loughlin's view, mean that an agreement under that section could validly be employed for positive purposes (short of an outright gift to the planning authority) so long as any positive obligations placed upon a developer could be said to be related to the agreement's *overall* purpose of restricting or regulating the development or use of land. It should perhaps be said that the adoption of a purposive approach means, of course, that the interpretation of a particular provision is dependent upon the view one takes of the underlying purposes of the legislation. Views can very easily differ as to the purposes of the Planning Acts.

"For the purpose of restricting or regulating"

So far as the law of Scotland is concerned, there is no such general restriction as exists south of the border in relation to the enforcement of positive obligations relating to land, and subsection (2) of section 50 simply declares that an agreement which has been recorded in the Register of Sasines is to be enforceable by the planning authority against persons deriving title from the person with whom the agreement was entered into. It would seem, therefore, that in Scotland no questions of principle arise as to enforceability. The question of the type of obligation that can validly be included in a section 50 agreement is entirely a matter of the interpretation of section 50(1) and, in particular, of the meaning to be given to the phrase "for the purpose of restricting or regulating".

This is not a matter that has so far had to be considered in a direct way by the courts,[16] although the decision in *R. v. Gillingham*

---

[14] The former Master of the Rolls, Lord Denning, was perhaps the most forceful advocate of the "purposive" approach—see, e.g. *The Discipline of Law*, Chap. 2, in which he states: "The literal method is now completely out of date."

[15] The disagreement between the exponents of these rival methods of interpretation relates not only to the question of which method better achieves the basic objective of discovering the intention of Parliament, but also to the question of how "creative" a role judges should adopt in interpreting statutes.

[16] See however *Attorney-General v. Barnes Corporation and Ranelagh Club* [1939] Ch. 110, in which an agreement made under s.34 of the Town and Country Planning Act 1932 was challenged on the ground that it was permissive rather than restrictive. Under s.34 planning authorities were empowered to enter into agreements subjecting land to "conditions restricting the planning, development

Borough Council, ex p. F. Parham Ltd.[17] and the comment of Lloyd L.J. in *City of Bradford Metropolitan Council* v. *Secretary of State for the Environment*,[18] both relating to the exercise of discretion in this area (see *infra* and Chapter 5) are clearly relevant. The words "restricting" and "regulating" are not defined in the 1972 Act. One can therefore do little more than speculate as to how the courts would interpret the provision and, in particular, as to how far they would permit a planning authority to go in the direction of seeking to achieve positive planning objectives by means of a section 50 agreement. Whether in the end of the day a judge adopts a literal or a purposive approach to legislation, he will of necessity look fairly closely at the actual words used by Parliament and it therefore seems worthwhile to consider the meaning of the component parts of the phrase "for the purpose of restricting or regulating" before going on to consider the meaning of the phrase taken as a whole.

It seems clear that an agreement can only be said to "restrict" the development or use of land if it is of a negative character, in the sense that it imposes some prohibition or limitation upon what is to be done on the land or permits the doing of something subject to conditions or within certain limits. Thus, for example, provisions prohibiting the parking of vehicles or the dumping of mineral spoil on a particular site, or limiting the classes of persons who may occupy buildings, or providing for extinguishment of the use of a particular piece of land might all be said to "restrict" the development or use of land.

"Regulating" presents rather more difficulty. A search through several of the standard dictionaries reveals that the literal meaning of "regulate" is to "adjust" or "control" or "govern" or "cause to conform to a standard".[19] The word's meaning seems to overlap

---

or use thereof." In this case it was alleged that the particular agreement, which gave permission for the development of land subject to certain restrictions, was in reality permissive in that it imposed less severe restrictions than applied to neighbouring landowners, and that it could not therefore be said to "restrict" the planning of the land in question. The court held that the agreement came within the ambit of the statutory powers.

[17] [1988] J.P.L. 336.

[18] (1986) 53 P. & C.R. 55.

[19] *Shorter Oxford English Dictionary* (1978): to control, govern or direct by rule or regulation; to subject to guidance or restrictions; to adjust, in respect of time, quantity, etc. *Chambers Twentieth Century Dictionary* (1979): to control; to adapt or adjust continuously; to adjust by rule. *Collins Dictionary of the English Language* (1979): to adjust as required; control; to adjust so that it operates correctly; to bring into conformity with a rule, principle or usage. *Penguin English Dictionary* (1979): to govern by rule; put in order; control by law; cause to function accurately; cause to conform to a standard. See also *Stroud's Judicial*

with that of "restrict". In so far as they are distinguishable, "restrict" would seem to be concerned primarily with limiting what can be done, whereas "regulate" is concerned with ensuring that something is done in a particular way. A regulatory provision might, for example, control the phasing of development or limit the hours during which premises may be used (so that it causes the land to conform to a standard).

On this definition, a requirement that a developer should undertake some positive obligation such as a requirement that he construct a community centre, or make a financial contribution towards the cost of public services generally could not, of itself, be regarded as "restricting" or "regulating" the development or use of land. (This is not to say, however, that an agreement under section 50 may not validly include such requirements provided the main purpose of such agreement is regulatory. The extent to which a section 50 agreement may properly do so is considered later in this chapter.) Support for this interpretation of the words "restricting or regulating" can be obtained by contrasting the wording of section 50 with the wording of section 27(1)(a) of the 1972 Act. The latter provision, which empowers a planning authority to impose certain types of condition on a grant of planning permission, makes a distinction between conditions "regulating the development or use of any land under the control of the applicant" and conditions "requiring the carrying out of works on any such land". In other words, section 27(1)(a) suggests that there is a difference between "regulating" conditions and conditions which seek to impose positive obligations. If, therefore, Parliament had intended to confer positive powers under section 50, it could easily have said so specifically.[20]

Section 50(1) provides that an agreement may contain "incidental and consequential provisions (including provisions of a financial character)". It is not likely that a court would give these words a broad construction[21] and we therefore feel that they do not broaden

---

Dictionary of Words and Phrases; and *Words and Phrases Legally Defined*.

[20] As, *e.g.* it did in s. 9 of the Countryside (Scotland) Act 1981, which enables a planning authority and the Countryside Commission to enter into management agreements with any person having an interest in land "to do, or to secure the doing of, whatever in the opinion of the parties to the agreement may be necessary to preserve or enhance the natural beauty of the countryside or to promote the enjoyment of the countryside by the public." It is in this way made clear that positive obligations can be imposed on the parties to the agreement.

[21] See, *e.g. D. & J. Nicol* v. *Dundee Harbour Trustees*, 1915 S.C.(H.L.) 7. In *Attorney-General* v. *Fulham Corporation* [1921] 1 Ch. 440 it was held that a laundry service run by a local authority was not "incidental to or consequential upon" the authority's powers to establish wash-houses." See also *Meek* v. *Lothian*

the scope of the earlier part of section 50(1) in any substantial way.[22] In the context of a condition requiring the widening of a road outside the developers' site Lloyd L.J. said (*obiter*) in *City of Bradford Metropolitan Council* v. *Secretary of State for the Environment*[23] that he did

> "not accept [counsel's] submissions that the present condition could have been lawful if incorporated in a section 52 agreement. If the condition was manifestly unreasonable, and so beyond the powers of the planning authority to impose it, whether or not the developers consented, it must follow that it was also beyond the powers of the planning authority to include the condition as an 'incidental or consequential provision' of an agreement restricting or regulating the development or use of the land under section 52."

The learned Lord Justice does not make clear why this should be so.[24]

The scope of section 50(1)

The responses to our first questionnaire survey in 1982 indicated that some Scottish planning authorities were chary of including in a section 50 agreement any obligation of a positive nature. We do not subscribe to this very narrow interpretation of the scope of section 50. It seems to us that the question that has to be asked in every case is whether the agreement, taken as a whole, could properly be said to have been made "for the purpose of restricting or regulating the development or use" of land. It seems to us that there is no bar to the inclusion in a section 50 agreement of obligations which are positive in character; the agreement must not, however, have as its sole or main purpose the achievement of some objective of a positive nature.[25] As Malcolm Grant put it: "Provided that the main clear purpose of an agreement is to restrict or regulate use or development, that purpose may be achieved through positive or negative consequential or incidental terms."[26] It may sometimes be possible to avoid potential problems by

---

Regional Council, 1980 S.L.T. (Notes) 61 ("'incidental to' should be applied with a narrow meaning and not as equivalent to 'in connection with'").

[22] It might in fact be asked whether these words add anything at all to s. 50(1)—see Chap. 1 (above).

[23] (1986) 53 P. & C.R. 55.

[24] See p. 36 *infra*.

[25] A literal view of s. 50(1) would therefore seem to lead to a conclusion broadly similar to that reached by Loughlin (*supra*) on a "purposive" interpretation of the English legislation.

[26] Paper presented to a conference on June 6, 1979, quoted in (1979) 251 E.G. 1262.

ensuring that particular provisions are worded in a negative way. SDD Circular 22/1984 states:

> "As to the question of whether an obligation of a positive nature can be imposed by way of a section 50 agreement, such agreements are 'for the purpose of restricting or regulating the development or use of the land'. While these words suggest a restrictive connotation, by taking a broad view of the purpose of the development proposed as a whole the inclusion of such obligations on the basis that their underlying overall purpose is restrictive in regulating the development itself may be justified. Such obligations might relate to the provision of car parking or open space . . . or might provide for housing as part of an office development, or secure the retention or restoration of a building which is of architectural or historical importance, but is not listed. Incidental and consequential provisions (including provisions of a financial character) which are considered necessary or expedient for the purposes of the agreement may also be included."

Whether, read as a whole, a particular agreement can be said to be restrictive or regulatory of the development or use of land is a question which will depend very largely on the terms of the agreement and generalisations on the question would appear to be unsafe. We would, however, make two comments.

First of all, it is often suggested that an agreement which imposes on a developer an obligation to provide or to make a financial contribution towards the cost of providing sewers, roads, open spaces and so on beyond those required by a proposed development cannot be construed as restricting or regulating the development or use of land. Such a suggestion fails to distinguish two separate but related questions. The first is whether such an agreement may be said to restrict or regulate the development or use of the land on which such provision is to be made; the second is whether such a requirement may properly influence a decision on a planning application for development to which it is not related. The first question falls to be answered within the four corners of the agreement itself. In *R. v. Gillingham Borough Council, ex p. F. Parham Ltd.*,[27] for example, Roch J. indicated that an agreement in which a developer undertook to construct on land under his control a road required not for his proposed development but to facilitate the continuous and progressive development of neighbouring land would have been an agreement entered into for the purpose of permanently restricting the use of the land on which the road was to be built. Of course, such a requirement also touches on the second question. Although such an agreement may

---

[27] [1988] J.P.L. 336.

be said to be restrictive of the use of land, where it is linked to a planning application other considerations also come into play. The other considerations relating to the planning authority's exercise of discretion are discussed in Chapter 5.

Our second comment is that difficult questions appear to arise in connection with agreements which seek to impose upon a developer an obligation to provide or to make a financial contribution towards all or part of the cost of providing sewers, roads, open spaces and so on.[28] In practice, agreements obliging developers to provide infrastructure or to contribute towards its cost are increasingly common in Scotland (see Chapter 8)[29] and are very common south of the border. Yet to what extent can such agreements properly be said to "restrict or regulate the development or use of land"? It may be legitimate regulation to prescribe certain consequences or actions to be taken in the event of certain things being done or not done.[30] If, for example, an agreement provided that a development was not to be occupied until such time as adequate provision had been made to cope with sewage resulting from the development or traffic generated by it, that provision could be said to be regulatory.[31]

It is questionable whether there is any real distinction between this last type of agreement and one which specifically provides that the developer will, at his own expense and before the development is occupied, carry out the necessary works to cope with the sewage or traffic which will result from the development. Although the wording is more positive, the overall purpose of both agreements is the same. They aim to ensure that the development is adequately drained and served by roads or, put another way, they seek to ensure that the development conforms to a certain standard.

Exactly the same purpose would also be achieved by an agreement which required the developer to meet all or part of the local authority's costs in providing the necessary work. Yet it appears that such provision may be outwith the scope of section 50. Subsection (1), which provides that an agreement may contain incidental and consequential financial provisions, implies that an

---

[28] See *City of Bradford Metropolitan Council* v. *Secretary of State for the Environment* (1986) 53 P. & C.R. 55.

[29] And see J. Rowan-Robinson and M. G. Lloyd, *Land Development and the Infrastructure Lottery* (T. & T. Clark, Edinburgh, 1988), Chap. 4.

[30] See letter from F. W. Hayes in [1979] J.P.L. 166.

[31] This is the sort of use which Dobry seems to have envisaged for agreements. See "Review of the Development Control System. Final Report," para. 7.71. And see now *Grampian Regional Council* v. *City of Aberdeen District Council* 1984 S.L.T. 197.

agreement cannot contain as its main provision an obligation of a financial nature.[32] However, although the words "restricting or regulating" have a restrictive connotation, if the object of a financial contribution is to secure the regulation of development and this is recited in the agreement, it may be possible to describe the obligation to make a contribution as consequential to the main purpose of the agreement, regulation of the development.

The propriety of seeking financial contributions appears to have given rise to some uncertainty at ministerial level. In 1974 the Secretary of State for the Environment expressed the view that agreements between planning authorities and developers about contributions to the cost of infrastructure could be made under the statutory powers which were then in operation.[33] However, the minister appears to have thought that the Planning Act powers on their own would not suffice for such agreements. He said that agreements of this kind might be made under section 52 of the Town and Country Planning Act 1971, and section 111 of the Local Government Act 1972.[34] Like section 69 of the Local Government (Scotland) Act 1973, section 111 of the 1972 Act empowers a local authority to do anything incidental to the discharge of its functions. Section 69 is considered in Chapter 9. Now SSD Circular 22/1984 indicates that section 50 agreements may encompass developers' contributions to infrastructure costs although attention is also drawn to section 69 of the 1973 Act as enabling "agreements to be made, which would not have to be limited in their purpose to restricting or regulating the development or use of land, for the payment of money or the transfer of assets to a local authority where this would facilitate the discharge of the functions of the authority."[35]

It seems to us unfortunate that, on our view of the scope of subsection (1), section 50 does not confer complete contractual freedom on the parties to an agreement. We think that the power in subsection (1) of section 50 is, as a result, less useful than it

---

[32] We are very conscious of the fact that we are here raising doubts about the competency of some agreements which seek to achieve objectives—contributions by developers to infrastructure costs—which virtually everyone seems to agree are useful and "morally" acceptable. And see *City of Bradford Metropolitan Council* v. *Secretary of State for the Environment* (1986) 53 P. & C.R. 55.

[33] See also DoE Circulars 102/72, para. 9 and 122/73, Annex. A, paras. 14 and 15; and PAN 26, issued by SDD in February 1981. See also the *Report of the Working Party on Local Authority/Private Enterprise Partnership Schemes* (the Sheaf Committee) (HMSO, 1972), p. 13.

[34] 867 H.C. Deb. 3745 (27 January 1974). See also Jeffery Jowell, "Bargaining in Development Control" [1977] J.P.L. 414, at pp. 417–418.

[35] See also para. 10 of SDD Circular 22/1984.

could be—particularly if the limitations upon the use of section 50
mean that parties cannot always contract freely over the provision
of, or contributions towards the cost of, infrastructure. It may well
be that these constraints are in part due to the concern of the
draftsman of the English legislation with restrictive covenants and
the fact that the terms of the Scottish legislation followed the
English statute fairly closely. If that is so, there is perhaps some
irony in the fact the powers available to English planning authorities
were substantially widened in 1974[36] but that no action was felt
necessary in relation to the Scottish legislation.

It should perhaps be said that both narrower and wider views
of the scope of section 50(1) have been advanced. For example,
in *City of Bradford Metropolitan Council* v. *Secretary of State for
the Environment*[37] Lloyd L.J., with whose opinion the other two
judges concurred, said (*obiter*) that:

> "practice under section 52, convenient and beneficial though it
> undoubtedly is, may have gone beyond what the strict language of
> the section demands. We were told that such agreements are now
> very common, much commoner than they used to be. It may be that
> in some future case it will be necessary for the court to consider the
> extent of the powers of planning authorities to enter into agreements
> under section 52."

He went on to suggest that an agreement under which a developer
undertook "unreasonable"[38] requirements might be invalid.

On the other hand, in the debates on the Town and Country
Planning Bill of 1947 the Lord Chancellor suggested that the
purposes for which the Bill's provisions on agreements might be
employed were very wide. He said[39] that agreements might deal,

> "with many various sorts of things—for instance, with waiver of
> claims for compensation for injurious affection in respect of certain
> lands on condition that no claims were made by the authorities for
> betterment in respect of development of other land; for gifts of land
> in consideration of permission to develop other land; for permitting
> public right of access to private lands in consideration of permission
> to develop other land; for granting permission to develop or redevelop

---

[36] By s. 126 of the Housing Act 1974. See now s. 33 of the Local Government
(Miscellaneous Provisions) Act 1982 (*supra*).

[37] (1986) 53 P. & C.R. 55 (see p. 36 *infra*).

[38] See also *R.* v. *Gillingham Borough Council, ex p. F. Parham Ltd.* [1988] J.P.L.
336. Tests of "reasonableness" are laid down in SDD Circular 22/1984 (see
pp. 140–145 *infra*) and DoE Circular 22/83 (the latter being referred to by Lloyd
L.J. in the course of his judgment in *City of Bradford Metropolitan Council* v.
Secretary of State for the Environment) (*supra*).

[39] 149 H.L. Deb. 642 (30 June 1947).

land on condition that the value of the works was discounted in computing the consideration on a subsequent purchase of the property by the authority."[40]

---

[40] We are somewhat doubtful as to whether an agreement providing for a gift of land in consideration of permission to develop other land could ever be regarded as being "for the purpose of restricting or regulating the development or use" of land. Some of the other types of agreement mentioned by the Lord Chancellor may be at the margin of regulation, but in appropriate circumstances probably could be said to come within the scope of the statutory power.

CHAPTER 4

"DEVELOPMENT OR USE" OF LAND

Section 50(1) enables planning agreements to be made for the purpose of restricting or regulating "the development or use" of land.

Research carried out in both England and Scotland shows that most planning agreements are related in some way to the development control functions of planning authorities.[1] The purposes for which agreements have been employed in Scotland are discussed in Chapter 8 of this book. Agreements have been used for a great variety of purposes. They may be used, for example, to duplicate or supplement conditions on planning permissions or as a substitute for such conditions (perhaps because of uncertainty about the legality of particular types of condition or because agreements can be more effectively enforced), to regulate matters which would not be subject to ordinary planning control, to achieve modification or cessation of development which was originally unauthorised, to extinguish existing rights or to transfer infrastructure costs to a developer.

It is clear that in the great majority of cases agreements are linked in fairly direct fashion to an application for planning permission, though the subject-matter of the agreement may well be something that was not included in the application for permission originally made. In return for planning permission to develop a particular site, a developer may be prepared, for example, to agree to the extinguishment of an existing authorised use or to the demolition of buildings on another site. The *Beaconsfield* case,[2] for example, arose out of an application for planning permission to build a bungalow on farm land. It was agreed that if the bungalow were erected, an existing farm house would be demolished.

[1] See, in particular Jeffrey Jowell, "Bargaining in Development Control" [1977] J.P.L. 414; J. N. Hawke "Planning Agreements in Practice" [1981] J.P.L. 5 and 86; and (for Scotland) the two unpublished theses mentioned in the bibliography to this book (App. 3) and the responses to the questionnaires we sent to Scottish planning authorities in 1982 and 1987.

[2] *Beaconsfield District Council* v. *Gams* (1974) 234 E.G. 749 and (1976) 237 E.G. 657. See Anthony P. Levings, "Planning by Agreement—the Beaconsfield Case" [1975] J.P.L. 704.

Planning agreements can, however, be used for wider purposes. Section 50 encompasses any development or *use* of land. It is therefore perfectly possible for an agreement to restrict or regulate matters which do not amount to "development" within the meaning of section 19 of the 1972 Act.[3] If, for example, a planning authority wished to ensure that a wilderness area or a mixed woodland was not lost as a result of agricultural or forestry operations (which are generally outside the scope of planning control), an agreement could provide a means of restricting or regulating such operations. A section 50 agreement might also offer a solution where a planning authority did not wish the owner or occupier of premises to be able to take advantage of the Use Classes Order[4]; where, for example, a planning authority believed there was a danger that a shop presently performing an essential service in providing for local needs might be used in future for some less essential purpose such as the sale of antiques or souvenirs for the tourist trade, they might seek to obviate the possibility of such a change by means of a section 50 agreement. A development or use of land which would not be subject to planning control because it is "permitted development" in terms of the General Development Order[5] can also be regulated by means of a section 50 agreement.

However, unless a landowner requires planning permission from the planning authority or the authority possess some other bargaining counter, there may well be problems in persuading the landowner to enter into an agreement restricting the development or use of land. Section 50 permits a planning authority to offer a financial inducement to a landowner. Telling[6] cites an example of a planning authority agreeing to bear the expense of repairs to a windmill in Kent in return for undertakings by the owner to restrict the use of a property to agricultural and private residential purposes and to allow members of the public to visit it. Alternatively, a planning authority might offer services such as assistance with the maintenance of a mixed woodland in order to induce a landowner to enter into an agreement.

The enactment of the Countryside (Scotland) Act 1981 may mean that there is less reason to use section 50 of the 1972 Act

---

[3] *Cf. City of London Corporation* v. *Secretary of State for the Environment* (1972) 23 P. & C.R. 169.
[4] The Town and Country Planning (Use Classes) (Scotland) Order 1973 has the effect of removing certain changes of use from the ambit of planning control.
[5] Under the Town and Country Planning (General Development) (Scotland) Order 1981 planning permission is granted for development falling within any of the 22 classes of development specified in Sched. 1 to the Order.
[6] *Planning Law and Procedure* (7th ed.), p. 189.

for the purpose of making agreements relating to countryside matters (see Chapter 9 below).[7] Management agreements under the 1981 Act can, however, only be used for the purposes of preserving or enhancing the appearance of the countryside or promoting its enjoyment by the public. Section 50 of the 1972 Act is not so restricted in its scope.

In *R. v. Gillingham Borough Council, ex p. F. Parham Ltd.*[8] Roch J. interpreted the power to restrict or regulate the *use* of land by agreement in a broad way (see Chapter 5). He considered that an agreement which required a developer to provide a road on land within his control, needed not for the proposed development but to facilitate the continuous and progressive development of neighbouring land, would be an agreement entered into for the purpose of permanently restricting the use of the land.

---

[7] See also s. 16 of the Local Government and Planning (Scotland) Act 1982 as regards agreements dealing with the provision of recreational facilities.
[8] [1988] J.P.L. 336.

CHAPTER 5

AGREEMENTS AND THE PLANNING AUTHORITY'S DISCRETION

"[T]he practice under section 52 [of the Town and Country Planning Act 1971, similar in its terms to section 50 of the Scottish Act of 1972], convenient and beneficial though it undoubtedly is, may have gone beyond what the strict language of the section justifies."
(Lloyd L.J. in *City of Bradford Metropolitan Council* v. *Secretary of State for the Environment*[1].)

FROM the point of view of the planning authority, one of the attractions of "planning by agreement" is that it enables the authority to broaden the scope of its development control powers. In particular, it is widely believed that planning authorities can, by means of agreements, get round some of the limitations and uncertainties connected with planning conditions. In this context account must now be taken of the decision in *R.* v. *Gillingham Borough Council, ex p. F. Parham Ltd.*[2] and of dicta in *City of Bradford Metropolitan Council* v. *Secretary of State for the Environment* (*infra*). Planning authorities clearly have a wide discretion to enter into agreements under section 50 and a further wide discretion as to the content of any such agreement, but there are, inevitably, certain legal constraints.

Planning purposes

In the first place, since the power to make agreements under section 50 is conferred by the planning legislation, it seems reasonable to suppose that such agreements should be entered into for a "planning" purpose. This was confirmed by Roch J. in *Gillingham*. "The first requirement," he said, "for a valid condition, namely, that it should be imposed for a planning purpose, and not for some ulterior one or improper purpose obviously applied to section 52 agreements. It would be undesirable to permit a practice whereby section 52 agreements were entered into as a condition

---

[1] (1986) 53 P. & C.R. 55.
[2] [1988] J.P.L. 336.

33

precedent to the granting of planning permission to achieve objectives other than planning objectives." It is clear, however, that the scope of "planning purposes" is wide. In *Stringer* v. *Minister of Housing and Local Government*[3] Cooke J. commented: "In principle, it seems to me that any consideration which relates to the use and development of land is capable of being a planning consideration." On this view, the requirement that an agreement must have a "planning" purpose would not seem to impose much of a constraint. However, somewhat narrower views of the legislation's scope have sometimes been expressed. In *David Lowe & Sons* v. *Burgh of Musselburgh*,[4] for example, the First Division of the Court of Session apparently considered that the planning legislation was not sufficiently broad to permit a planning authority to concern itself with questions relating to the ownership and disposal of land.[5] It is therefore conceivable that an agreement which sought to prevent division of the ownership of land might be open to question. On the other hand, in *Gillingham*, Roch J. declared that a planning agreement which required a developer to construct on land under his control (but without reservation of a ransom strip) a road required, not for his development but to facilitate the continuous and progressive development of neighbouring land, would serve a planning purpose.

Material considerations

More significantly, if an agreement relates in some way to the exercise by a planning authority of their development control powers, then the agreement is likely to have to be confined to dealing with "material considerations". The reason for this is that sections 26 and 84 of the 1972 Act stipulate the matters which may be taken into account by a planning authority in determining a planning application or in deciding whether or not to take enforcement action. The principal such matters are the development plan and "any other material considerations."[6] In deciding whether or not to grant permission or to serve an enforcement

---

[3] [1970] 1 W.L.R. 1281. See also *Westminster City Council* v. *Great Portland Estates plc* [1984] 3 W.L.R. 1035 *per* Lord Scarman.

[4] 1974 S.L.T. 5.

[5] It seems to us that this is an unduly narrow view of the objectives which a planning authority may legitimately seek to achieve. The views expressed in *David Lowe* appear to be inconsistent with the decision of the House of Lords in *Fawcett Properties Ltd.* v. *Buckingham County Council* [1961] A.C. 636.

[6] In determining a planning application a planning authority are also required to take account of any representations received in response to publicity and consultation, the regional report (together with the Secretary of State's comments on it) and the needs of disabled persons.

notice the authority may well be influenced by the outcome of any negotiations over a planning agreement. Indeed, a successful conclusion to the negotiation is often in practice a condition precedent to a grant of permission. Such agreements must, therefore, either be the consequence of a policy or proposal in the development plan or a "material consideration".

Agreements which are the consequence of a policy or proposal in the development plan are exceptional at present, but a number of examples have been noted in England.[7] The response to our questionnaires showed few examples in Scotland. The Loch Lomond Subject Plan contains a policy statement in these terms: "The Local Authorities will enter into agreements with landowners to facilitate public access in suitable locations in accordance with the objectives of the policy area." Apart from this, two other authorities stated that they were promoting policies to secure the provision of adequate amenity areas in future large scale developments.

The expression "material consideration" would appear to be narrower in scope than "planning consideration". In *Stringer* Cooke J. said: "Whether a particular consideration falling within that broad class [i.e. of planning considerations] is material in any given case will depend on the circumstances." The implication here is that material considerations are those considerations relating to the use and development of land which arise out of, or are relevant to, the matter in hand. This would seem to be another way of saying that such considerations must be "relevant" in the sense in which that term is understood in administrative law.[8] For example, the fact that a development proposal will require an extension to a sewage works would clearly be a material consideration which arguably could be dealt with by agreement. If, however, the planning authority are requiring the developer in the agreement not only to bear the cost of extending the sewage works to cope with the development but to cope with further expansion in other parts of the town and the grant of planning permission is dependent on agreement on this, then it is hard to see how that could be a material consideration. Future developments in other parts of the town do not arise from and are not relevant to

---

[7] See, *e.g.* M. Grant, "Developers' Contributions and Planning Gains: Ethics and Legalities"; [1978] J.P.L. 8; M. Loughlin, "Planning Gain: Law, Policy and Practice"; (1981) 1 Oxford Jo. of Legal Studies 61; and "Planning Gain," Report by the Property Advisory Group (HMSO, 1981).

[8] See *Associated Provincial Picture Houses Ltd.* v. *Wednesbury Corporation* [1948] 1 K.B. 223; and see, generally H. W. R. Wade, *Administrative Law* (Clarendon Press, 6th ed.), pp. 411–413.

the application in hand. Similar arguments would apply to a requirement in an agreement to provide a community centre or public open space. The important question here is whether the requirement arises from the proposal in question. If it does not, then it should not be allowed to influence the authority in its development control functions.[9]

This relation between the proposed development and the subject matter of any linked agreement is stressed by the SDD in their policy advice on the use of agreements in Circular 22/1984 (see Appendix 2). The Circular provides that one of the tests that has to be applied to section 50 agreements is,

"whether the extent of what is required or sought is fairly and reasonably related in scale and kind to the proposed development. Thus, while the developer may reasonably be expected to pay for or contribute to the cost of infrastructure which would not have been necessary but for his development, and while some public benefit may eventually accrue from this, his payments should be directly related in scale and kind to the benefit which the proposed development will derive from the facilities to be provided".

However, in R. v. *Gillingham Borough Council, ex p. F. Parham Ltd.*[10] Roch J. held that an obligation undertaken by a developer need not fairly and reasonably relate to the permitted development.

"Section 52 required that an agreement should be 'for the purpose of restricting or regulating the development or use of the land, either permanently or during such period as may be prescribed by the agreement'. Those words allowed a section 52 agreement to go beyond matters that fairly or reasonably related to the permitted development.[11] Section 52 agreements could encompass matters which restricted or regulated the use of the land. This was not surprising because there would be little point in enacting section 52 of the 1971 Act if section 52 agreements were confined to those matters which could be dealt with by way of conditions."

The agreement in issue in that case provided for the construction of a road extending some way beyond what was required for the permitted development. The section 52 agreement required the

---

[9] If this view is correct, a planning authority may have to exercise considerable caution when, at the time of making a planning application, a developer offers to enter into a s. 50 agreement. There is a danger that the authority may in this fashion take some irrelevant matter into account.

[10] [1988] J.P.L. 336.

[11] Roch J. is referring here to the well-established test for planning conditions that they should be fairly and reasonably related to the subject matter of the planning application (*Newbury District Council* v. *Secretary of State for the Environment* [1981] A.C. 578; *British Airports Authority* v. *Secretary of State for Scotland* 1979 S.C. 200; 1979 S.L.T. 197).

construction of a "T" junction whereas, for the purpose of the proposed development, namely the erection of dwelling-houses, a simple bend would have sufficed. Roch J. found that the purpose of requiring the construction of the "T" junction was not for the benefit of the houses to be built, but to facilitate the progressive and continuous development of adjoining land. It was not, however, argued that the condition was invalid for this reason.

It is difficult to reconcile the decision in *Gillingham* with the requirement in section 26(1) of the 1972 Act to have regard only to "material considerations" when determining a planning application. The grant of planning permission in *Gillingham* clearly turned on the willingness of the applicant to enter into the section 52 agreement, the planning committee having indicated that permission would be refused in the event of the applicant being unwilling to proceed. Yet it is difficult to see how agreement to provide a road not required for the proposed development could be said to be relevant or material to the decision on the planning application. It must be very doubtful whether unwillingness to assume such an obligation in an agreement could have supported a refusal of the application. While we respectfully agree with Roch J. that obligations in an agreement may go beyond matters that are fairly or reasonably related to the planning application, we think that, if the subsequent planning permission is to avoid the risk of challenge, such obligations must nevertheless be relevant or material to the proposed development. In determining a planning application, a planning authority may not go beyond matters that are relevant or material to that application.

This is not to suggest that agreements linked to a planning application must be confined to those matters which may be the subject of conditions. There is a range of matters, particularly the provision of supporting infrastructure, which for one reason or another may be beyond the proper scope of conditions[12] but which are clearly material to a decision on the application and may properly be the subject of agreement.

Nonetheless, unsatisfactory as the *Gillingham* decision may be in this respect, it would seem that, unless and until it is overturned, the ability to negotiate planning agreements may be regarded by planning authorities as an opportunity to substantially extend their development control powers. This would seem to leave SDD Circular 22/1984 somewhat in disarray.

---

[12] See, *e.g. M. J. Shanley Ltd. (in liquidation)* v. *Secretary of State for the Environment* [1982] J.P.L. 380, and *Birnie* v. *Banff County Council* 1954 S.L.T. (Sh.Ct.) 90.

In addition to ignoring irrelevant considerations, the planning authority must also ensure that the advantages they envisage arising from an agreement do not cause them to ignore other relevant considerations. Failure in this respect will lay their decision on the planning application open to challenge. An illustration of this is provided by the decision in *J. J. Steeples* v. *Derbyshire County Council.*[13] In that case Webster J. held that the terms of an agreement between the planning authority and a developer would suggest to a reasonable man that there would be a real likelihood of bias on the part of the authority when they came to determine the subsequent and related planning application. The decision on the application was accordingly held not to have complied with the requirements of natural justice. The question of whether a planning permission which is linked to a section 50 agreement could be challenged on the grounds of bias is considered later. The point to be made here is that where such an agreement exists then the planning authority must be scrupulously fair in determining the application if it is to avoid a challenge on the ground that it has ignored relevant considerations.[14]

It would seem that if the parties to a planning appeal indicate their willingness to enter into an agreement, that is a matter which the Secretary of State will have to take into account in reaching his decision.[15]

Reasonableness

We said at the beginning of this chapter that planning authorities have wide discretion regarding section 50 agreements but that there are inevitably certain legal constraints. So far we have

---

[13] [1981] J.P.L. 582; and see comment in 1982 S.P.L.P. 19.

[14] It may be said, however, that in *Jones* v. *Secretary of State for Wales* (1974) 72 L.G.R. 583 Lord Denning quoted with apparent approval para. 64 of Planning Bulletin No. 1 (MHLG, 1962), in which advice on local authority/private enterprise partnership schemes is given in the following terms:

"Provided the local planning authority in putting forward the comprehensive development area have had due regard to their statutory duty in regard to the planning of the area, the existence of prior financial and/or other arrangements between the local authority and a prospective developer or developers would not in the Minister's view affect the *vires* of the proposal."

[15] See *McLaren* v. *Secretary of State for the Environment* [1981] J.P.L. 423, and *Sutton London Borough Council* v. *Secretary of State for the Environment*, Court of Appeal, 2 March 1987, unreported but summarised at [1988] J.P.L. 281. *Cf.* however *Tarmac Properties* v. *Secretary of State for Wales* (1976) 33 P. & C.R. 103; [1976] J.P.L. 576 in which it was held that the Secretary of State had not acted unreasonably in not taking into account an agreement which had been drafted but never executed by the parties.

examined two possible constraints. There is, however, a third. It is well established that discretion must not be exercised unreasonably.[16] "Unreasonable" here has a special meaning. In *Gillingham* Roch J. said:

> "A decision was not unreasonable unless properly described as being irrational, or it was a decision which in itself indicated bad faith, or that it had been reached for some improper motive, or (to use a colloquial phrase used by Lord Scarman) that the person or body taking the decision had taken leave of his or its senses. It was not sufficient that the court would not, on the material that was apparently considered by the decision-maker, have reached that decision, nor was it sufficient that the court felt strongly that the choice made was the wrong one."

Important comments about the application of this constraint on the use of planning agreements were made by Lloyd L.J. in the Court of Appeal in *City of Bradford Metropolitan Council* v. *Secretary of State for the Environment*[17]. The other two judges agreed with his judgment.

A local planning authority had imposed on a grant of planning permission a condition requiring that, before the dwellings authorised by the permission were occupied, road widening works should be carried out in accordance with the submitted plans. The Court of Appeal held the condition to be *ultra vires* but in the course of his judgment Lloyd L.J. said (*obiter*) that he was not prepared to accept:

> "that the present condition would have been lawful if incorporated in a section 52 agreement. If the condition was manifestly unreasonable, and so beyond the powers of the planning authority to impose it, whether or not the developers consented, it must follow that it was also beyond the powers of the planning authority to include the condition as an 'incidental or consequential provision' of an agreement restricting or regulating the development or use of the land under section 52.

> "That is not to say that this might not have been a case for a more limited agreement under section 52. A contribution towards the cost of [road] widening . . . might well have been reasonable due to the increased use of the road resulting from the development, and the benefit to the occupiers of the residential development: see Circular

---

[16] See *Associated Provincial Picture Houses Ltd.* v. *Wednesbury Corporation* [1948] 1 K.B. 223; *Hall & Co. Ltd.* v. *Shoreham-by-Sea UDC* [1964] 1 W.L.R. 240; and *City of Bradford Metropolitan Council* v. *Secretary of State for the Environment* (1986) 53 P. & C.R. 55. See also H.W.R. Wade, *supra.*, Chap. 12.

[17] (1986) 53 P. & C.R. 55.

22/83 'Planning Gain', where the considerations are well set out . . .
But I need not pursue that consideration further. For there is all the
difference in the world between a provision of a section 52 agreement
requiring a contribution from a developer towards the cost of widening
the highway, and a provision which requires the entire works to be
carried out at his risk and expense."

A number of aspects of Lloyd L.J.'s statement might be questioned.
He suggests, firstly, that if a condition is unreasonable it has to
follow that the provisions of the condition cannot be included in
an agreement under section 52. As Colin Crawford points out,[18]
if this formulation is correct, then the only advantage that a section
50 agreement would have over a condition would lie in the greater
ease of enforcing an agreement.

While Lloyd L.J. suggests that an agreement requiring a developer to carry out road widening would be *ultra vires*, a more
limited agreement might have been competent—that is an agreement under which a *contribution* to the cost of road widening was
made. As Crawford states, this confuses the situation further,
although it would appear that what was being suggested was simply
that the obligation should be in proportion to the consequences
of the development.

The wording of section 52 of the 1971 Act is totally different
from that of section 29 which, like section 26 of the Scottish Act,
empowers a planning authority to impose on a grant of planning
permission such conditions as they think fit. It would have been
helpful to know why the learned Lord Justice considered that a
planning authority's powers under section 52 should be equated
to their powers under section 29 to impose conditions on planning
permissions. As Grant points out,[19] there was no consideration of
the different purpose and wording of each of these provisions.

Nor was there, says Grant, any consideration of the relationship
between section 52 and authorities' normal contractual powers.
He states: "Merely because a condition may be in breach of the
principles judicially constructed as a safeguard to the use of power
under s.29 does not require that it must also be in breach of s.52."
First, an agreement can only come about under section 52 if both
parties consent. It is therefore very different from the power to
impose conditions. Then section 52 "does not necessarily create
any new contractual power to enter into agreements with developers, . . . merely a right to enforce an agreement which satisfies the
requirements of the section against successors in title to the land."

---

[18] (1987) 20 S.P.L.P. 20.
[19] *Urban Planning Law* (1st Supplement), pp. 359–374.

Grant further points out that an agreement may typically provide for the developer paying road costs so as to allow the building of a road to a proposed housing estate earlier than would otherwise be possible. The agreement provides, he says:

> "a flexible means of reconciling the differing requirements of the private and public sector in providing off-site infrastructure . . . To impose upon it a doctrinal test of reasonableness would cut across this beneficial usage, and deprive developers of their least unsatisfactory method of buying forward infrastructure."

The observations of Lloyd L.J. on reasonableness and the use of agreements in *City of Bradford Metropolitan Council* were considered in *Gillingham*. There Roch J. accepted that a section 52 agreement "had to be such as a reasonable planning authority, duly appreciating its statutory duties, could properly have imposed". Comparing the facts with those in the *Bradford* case one might have expected the agreement in *Gillingham* to be categorised as equally unreasonable. However, as Purdue comments:[20]

> "Finally, it is significant that while Roch J referred to the *Bradford* case, he studiously avoided the obvious question of whether the planning agreement offended the principle of unreasonableness by containing a positive undertaking to extend the existing highway. In the *Bradford* case Lloyd LJ seemed to consider that a provision requiring the widening of a highway entirely by and at the cost of the developer would be beyond the scope of an agreement under s52. Roch J did not go into this aspect of the *Bradford* case and seemed to think that its ratio was that the condition was unreasonable because it related to land not in the applicant's control."

Of the submission that the agreement and the related grant of planning permission were unreasonable, Roch J. said that there was no hint that the planning authority had not followed procedures which were fair to the developers and to adjoining owners. Nor was there any suggestion that the authority were motivated by some improper or ulterior motive. The point to which the road should be extended was only one detail in the overall question of whether or not planning permission should be granted for the development proposed. Relevant factors had been taken into account. Roch J. concluded that the decision was a "decision which it was open to [the planning authority] to reach on the material before them, taking into consideration all those matters which they were required by the law to consider." It had not been established that the decision was irrational or unreasonable.

---

[20] [1988] J.P.L. 336, p. 343.

Conclusion

From what we have said in this chapter there would seem to be good grounds for suggesting that the decisions in the *Bradford* and *Gillingham* cases raise more issues than they resolve. In particular, the courts do not seem satisfactorily to have addressed the difficult relationship between the agreement and the related planning permission; nor have they given any clear guidance how a test of reasonableness should be applied to obligations about which the parties are in agreement. As Lloyd L.J. acknowledged in *Bradford*, "[t]he fact that the applicant had suggested a condition or consented to its terms was, of course, likely to be powerful evidence that the condition was not unreasonable on the facts, since, as in the case of any commercial transaction, the parties were usually the best judges of what was reasonable." He did, however, go on to observe that the analogy with a commercial transaction was not complete as the "parties" to a planning application were not in the same sort of position.

It might have been better if planning authorities had been left with freedom to contract for planning purposes. Attention in terms of safeguards could simply have focused on the related planning decision and the well-established principles for ensuring a proper exercise of discretion. To attempt to import those principles into the field of agreements seems highly problematic.

CHAPTER 6

AGREEMENTS AND THE FETTERING OF POWERS

Introduction

ONE aspect of the *ultra vires* doctrine which is very relevant in connection with planning agreements is the general common law rule of statutory interpretation that public bodies which have been entrusted with the exercise of statutory powers and duties "cannot enter into any contract or take action incompatible with the due exercise of their powers or the discharge of their duties."[1] A public authority cannot, as it were, disable themselves by contract from exercising their powers or from performing their statutory duties. The authority's "paramount duty is to preserve their own freedom to decide in every case as the public interest requires at the time."[2] It would seem that a contract made in violation of this principle is void.[3]

Planning authorities exercise important and far-reaching statutory functions. It therefore seems to be a matter of some significance to consider how far such authorities can, by means of an agreement under section 50 of the 1972 Act, validly restrict the future exercise of their powers. Can they, for example, in exchange for obligations undertaken by the other party to an agreement undertake that they will refrain from taking enforcement action in respect of a particular unauthorised development?

Not only may the extent to which powers can be fettered by means of a section 50 agreement be a matter of concern to planning authorities: this question may be of even greater concern to those considering entering into an agreement with an authority. In *Windsor & Maidenhead Royal Borough Council* v. *Brandrose Investments*[4] Walton J. said that if it were not possible for a planning authority to contract not to exercise its statutory powers in the future or to contract as to the manner in which it would

---

[1] *Birkdale District Electricity Supply Company* v. *Southport Corporation* [1926] A.C. 355, *per* Lord Birkenhead at p. 364.

[2] Wade, *Administrative Law* (6th ed.), p. 375.

[3] See C. Turpin, *Government Contracts*, p. 23. It would seem that the public body cannot be estopped from itself founding upon the invalidity of any such "contract" it has entered into—see *Rhyl U.D.C.* v. *Rhyl Amusements* [1959] 1 W.L.R. 465.

[4] [1981] 1 W.L.R. 1083.

exercise its powers in the future, then "the attractions from the point of view of the land-owner of entering into any such agreement would be minimal." This is perhaps overstating the case—a landowner may often consider it advantageous to enter a section 50 agreement which imposes obligations upon him but contains no undertakings on the part of the planning authority—but it is clear that anyone negotiating an agreement with an authority will be concerned to ensure that the agreement is not *ultra vires* as imposing unlawful restrictions upon the authority.

The practical significance of this issue to the concerns of this book may be illustrated by the decision in *Stringer* v. *Minister of Housing and Local Government*.[5] In that case an undertaking was given by a planning authority under powers contained in a Private Act[6] that they would, "within the limits of their powers," discourage development in a particular area. The purpose of the undertaking was to safeguard the operation of the Jodrell Bank radio telescope. Cooke J. held that this agreement was inconsistent with the proper performance of the planning authority's statutory duties. Under the planning legislation authorities are required, in considering an application for planning permission, to have regard to the development plan and to "any other material considerations." It was held that the effect of the agreement was to bind the authority to disregard considerations relevant to a planning application, considerations which, under the Act, the authority were obliged to take into account. Even though the parties to the agreement perhaps did not intend that it should be legally enforceable, each side intended, in Cooke J.'s view, to undertake its side of the bargain; he therefore held that the agreement was *ultra vires*.[7]

On the facts before him in *Stringer* Cooke J. had no difficulty in concluding that the planning authority had violated the principle that a public body cannot enter into any commitment which is incompatible with the proper exercise of its powers. However, the operation of this principle in practice can sometimes give rise to very difficult questions, some of which are considered below.

The principle that "incompatible" contracts are *ultra vires* is, of course, founded upon the presumption that Parliament cannot have intended that public bodies should be able, by agreement,

---

[5] [1970] 1 W.L.R. 1281.

[6] The report of the case does not specify the statutory powers under which this undertaking was given. However J. N. Hawke states ([1980] J.P.L. 386) that the agreement was made under powers conferred by the Cheshire County Council Act 1953 which were more restrictive than those in s. 52.

[7] Certain aspects of this decision are considered later in this book.

to disable themselves from carrying out their statutory responsibilities. However, if Parliament manifests an intention that public bodies such as planning authorities should be able to bind themselves in particular ways, there is, of course, no place for the operation of such a presumption. The most important question in the present context, therefore, is the extent to which authorities are empowered by section 50 of the 1972 Act to fetter the future exercise of their powers.

Section 50(3)

Subsection (3) of section 50 declares:

"Nothing in this section or in any agreement made thereunder shall be construed—
(a) as restricting the exercise, in relation to land which is the subject of any such agreement, of any powers exercisable by any Minister or authority under this Act so long as those powers are exercised in accordance with the development plan, or in accordance with any directions which may have been given by the Secretary of State as to the provisions to be included in such a plan; or
(b) as requiring the exercise of any such powers otherwise than as mentioned in paragraph (a) of this subsection."

In *Brandrose* it was held at first instance that an agreement under section 52 of the Town and Country Planning Act 1971 (subsection (3) of which is identical to the corresponding subsection of the Scottish Act of 1972) could validly impose some restriction upon the future exercise of statutory powers. Fox J. said that it seemed to him that "both paragraphs (a) and (b) in subsection (3) contemplate the existence, in consequence of a section 52 agreement, of fetters upon the powers of the local planning authority."[8]

The wording of subsection (3) of section 52 of the Town and Country Planning Act 1971 is described by Malcolm Grant as "remarkably obscure." He states that,

"the only way to read any sense into it is to construe it as containing a double negative, so that when it proclaims that nothing in any agreement is to be construed as restricting the exercise of any powers 'so long as those powers are exercised in accordance with the development plan' (or as *requiring* their exercise other than in that way), it means that the authority *may* bind itself as to the future exercise of the statutory powers unless and until they are exercised in accordance with the provisions of the development plan. If the

---

[8] p. 1089.

plan did not support the proposed exercise of powers, then it would first have to be amended."[9]

As Grant points out elsewhere[10] the legislative intention of Parliament accords with that construction of the statute. He states:

"But one important limitation remains, which is that an authority may not, as a general rule, enter into a contractual arrangement which has the effect of fettering the future exercise of a statutory discretion. Subsection (3) of s52 acknowledges the rule, by providing that nothing in the section or in any agreement made under it, should be construed as restricting the exercise of any powers conferred by the Act. In its original form in the 1947 Bill, the prohibition was absolute. But opposition members argued that, as it stood, the section offered no security to landowners that the authorities would keep their side of the bargain and not simply override agreements under their statutory powers. An amendment was therefore introduced, which added the words 'so long as the powers are exercised in accordance with the provisions of the development plan'. Although the subsection as finally enacted proceeds by way of a double negative, its intended effect must be to confer on authorities the power to restrict the future exercise of a statutory power, except where the power is to be exercised in accordance with the development plan."

Subsection (3) of section 52 of the 1971 Act came under judicial scrutiny in the *Brandrose* case which is considered later in this chapter.

Difficult questions can arise as to the extent to which powers can be lawfully fettered by means of a section 50 agreement and any attempt to assess the effect of section 50 would seem to necessitate some consideration of the general legal background against which it operates. Some aspects of the general law relating to the fettering of powers are considered briefly in the next part of this chapter.

Restricting future freedom

The law relating to contracts which have the effect of restricting in some way the future freedom of a public body is an area of enormous difficulty.[11] The principles to be applied are somewhat

---

[9] "The Planning After Effects of the *Brandrose* Decision," 1983 L.G.C. 768.
[10] *Urban Planning Law*, p. 368.
[11] Rather to our surprise, we were unable to find much detailed discussion of the problems in the textbooks and journals. See however, P. Rogerson, "On the Fettering of Public Powers" [1971] P.L. 288; J. M. Evans, *de Smith's Judicial Review of Administrative Action* (5th ed.) pp. 317–320: H. W. R. Wade, *Administrative Law* (6th ed.) pp. 388–401; J. D. B. Mitchell, *The Contracts of Public Authorities*; C. Turpin, *Government Contracts*, pp. 19–25.

ill-defined, the decision in the leading case, *Ayr Harbour Trustees*
v. *Oswald*,[12] is open to different interpretations; much appears to
depend on the facts of the individual case, widely divergent judicial
attitudes are to be seen in the courts' decisions[13] and it seems
impossible to reconcile all the decisions.

There are decisions and dicta which demonstrate that the courts
will sometimes be very concerned to ensure that public bodies
preserve intact their future freedom of action.[14] In *York Corporation* v. *Henry Leetham & Sons*,[15] for example, Russell J. stated
that the decision in the *Ayr* case and "many other cases" demonstrated "the incapacity of any body charged with statutory powers
to divest itself of such powers or to fetter itself in the use of such
powers."[16] Similarly, in *Ellice's Trustees* v. *Commissioners of the
Caledonian Canal*[17] the Lord Ordinary, Lord Stormonth-Darling,
said that a statutory body "can do nothing to disable themselves
or their successors from exercising at any time their full statutory
powers."

In the town planning field there are two cases—*Ransom & Luck
Ltd.* v. *Surbiton Borough Council*[18] and *Triggs* v. *Staines Urban
District Council*[19]—which provide good illustrations of the effect
of this restrictive approach to authorities' contractual undertakings.

In the judgments in *Ransom & Luck* there can perhaps be
discerned a very considerable reluctance on the part of the
members of the Court of Appeal to accept the possibility that a
planning authority might be able to "bargain away its statutory
powers of planning," conferred upon the authority "in the public
interest." In this case a local authority had entered into an
agreement under section 34 of the Town and Country Planning
Act 1932. The authority had, it was alleged, bound itself not to
exercise its statutory powers to restrict the future development of
the land which was the subject of the agreement.

---

[12] (1883) 10 R.(H.L.) 85: 8 App.Cas. 623.
[13] *Cf., e.g.*, the judgments in *Ransom & Luck* v. *Surbiton Borough Council* [1949]
Ch. 180 with Fox J.'s judgment in *Brandrose*.
[14] See, *e.g.* *York Corporation* v. *Henry Leetham & Sons* [1924] 1 Ch. 557; *William
Cory & Son* v. *London Corporation* [1951] 2 K.B. 476; and *Southend-on-Sea
Corporation* v. *Hodgson (Wickford) Ltd.* [1962] 1 Q.B. 416 (in which Lord
Parker C.J. declared: "There is a long line of cases . . . which lay down that a
public authority cannot by contract fetter the exercise of its discretion").
[15] *Supra.*
[16] Russell J.'s reasoning was, however, criticised in the House of Lords in *Birkdale
District Electricity Supply Company* v. *Southport Corporation* [1926] A.C. 355.
[17] (1904) 6 F. 325.
[18] [1949] Ch. 180.
[19] [1969] 1 Ch. 10.

Lord Greene M.R. said: "unless there is to be found somewhere in the statute statutory power to a planning authority to restrict or tie its hands in the matter of planning, no such power could exist." It was not likely, his Lordship thought, that Parliament "would do anything so unusual, so explosive, as to enable a planning authority to do that which all the principles laid down and observed by the courts and the legislature in regard to statutory duties of this kind forbid, namely to tie its hands and contract itself out of them."

Section 34 of the 1932 Act provided that where any landowner was willing to agree with a local authority that his land should be subjected to conditions restricting its planning, development or use, the authority might enter into an agreement with him to that effect. The Court of Appeal considered that the sole purposes of section 34 were to allow local authorities to accept undertakings from landowners and to enable authorities to enforce such undertakings: section 34 could not, the court held, be construed as empowering a local authority to restrict in any way its statutory powers.

In *Triggs* a local authority had entered into a complex agreement[20] with the owners of a sports ground. The agreement provided that so long as the land continued to be used as a private sports ground, the authority would not acquire the land under the powers conferred on them by the Town and Country Planning Act 1932. The council were, however, granted an option to acquire the land if it ceased to be used as a sports ground, but if the option was not exercised within a specified period, then the land was to be forever free from the council's power of acquisition and the landowners were to be free to develop it as they chose.

In court the local authority simply conceded that the agreement was unenforceable against them. Cross J. declared: "The difficulty which was overlooked by those who prepared the agreement was that the council could not effectively contract not to exercise its statutory powers or to abdicate its statutory duties."

The sweeping expressions of principle in cases such as *Ransom & Luck*, *York Corporation* and *Southend* might suggest that a contract which fetters public powers in any way is necessarily *ultra vires*. The true principle cannot, however, be nearly as broad as that. In order to carry out their functions, public bodies need to be able to make contracts, many of which will inevitably impose

---

[20] The report of the case does not make clear whether the agreement was, like the agreement in *Ransom & Luck*, made under s. 34 of the 1932 Act, but that Act was in force at the time the agreement was made.

some restriction on authorities' future freedom of action. This is, of course, especially true of bodies like local authorities which will often have a wide range of powers relating to the same subject matter. It would be impossible for a local authority to exercise one of its powers and at the same time retain complete freedom to exercise all its other powers. It clearly cannot be the law that every contract which is inconsistent with the future exercise of some power is on that account *ultra vires*. In Wade's words: "There will often be situations where a public authority must be at liberty to bind itself for the very purpose of exercising its powers effectively."[21]

The problem is that the courts have not provided any very clear guidelines as to how and where the line is to be drawn between, on the one hand, a contract which is an improper restriction of an authority's discretion and, on the other hand, a contract which is a legitimate exercise of that discretion. It is often said that the question which must be asked is whether the contract is compatible with the functions of the body in question.[22] The application of this test may be illustrated by reference to a number of cases.

In the *Ayr* case harbour trustees were constituted under the Ayr Harbour Improvement Act to modernise and improve the harbour. In acquiring land for this purpose, the trustees were prepared to accept a restriction in the conveyance reserving a private access. As Rogerson comments,[23] the effect of this undertaking would have been to frustrate the whole policy of the Act. The restriction was therefore held to be invalid, being incompatible with the statutory functions of the trustees.

Whether or not a contract is compatible with the functions of the body in question would seem to be a matter of fact to be determined in the circumstances of each case. In *British Transport Commission* v. *Westmorland County Council*[24] the House of Lords declined to accept the argument that there could be no dedication of a public right of way across an accommodation bridge over a railway line. The court adopted a more pragmatic approach. Was there a likelihood that such a dedication would interfere with the efficient operation of the railway? On the facts of the case, the court held that there was no such likelihood.

It is clear, also, that the test should not be applied too literally. In *Blake* v. *Hendon Corporation*[25] a local authority had exercised

---

[21] *Administrative Law* (6th ed.), p. 379.
[22] See, *e.g. Birkdale* (*supra*).
[23] P. Rogerson, "On the Fettering of Public Powers" [1971] P.L. 288 at p. 291.
[24] [1958] A.C. 126.
[25] [1962] Q.B. 283.

its statutory powers to dedicate land as a public park. It was argued
that the authority was not entitled to take this action because it
would then not be able to exercise another of its powers, the
power to let the land. That argument was rejected by the Court
of Appeal. As Devlin L.J. pointed out, it could have been argued
with just as much force that the authority could not let the land
because that would interfere with the statutory power of dedication.
To uphold such an argument would lead to the absurd result that
the authority could not lawfully exercise either power. The
important thing was to ascertain the primary purpose for which
the land was held. All other powers were to be considered
subordinate to that primary purpose and could only be exercised
to the extent that they were compatible with that purpose. In
Blake, the court held that the power to let the land was subordinate
to the primary purpose of the legislation which was to dedicate
land for public use.

A similar approach underlies the decision in *Stourcliffe Estates
Co. v. Bournemouth Corporation.*[26] In that case a local authority
had acquired land with a view to providing public gardens. In the
conveyance of the land the authority covenanted with the vendor
to limit the categories of buildings which might be erected on the
land. At a later date the authority decided under other statutory
powers, but in breach of the covenant, to construct public toilets
on the land. The court considered that the covenant did not in
any way preclude the authority from using the land for the purpose
for which it had been acquired. The covenant was not, therefore,
incompatible. It merely precluded the authority from exercising
certain ancillary and subsidiary powers, powers which did not have
to be used for the purpose for which the land had been acquired
but were permissive only. Although the local authority had specific
powers to construct toilets in public places, there was no obligation
on them to do so. As Buckley L.J. pointed out, it was not necessary
that the authority should with every piece of land they bought,
"acquire also the right to put a urinal there."[27]

The judgment of Sir John Pennycuick V.C. in *Dowty Boulton
Paul v. Wolverhampton Corporation*[28] is of particular interest in
connection with the powers of multi-function bodies like local
authorities, not least because Fox J. drew assistance from it in

---

[26] [1910] 2 Ch. 12. See also *Earl of Leicester* v. *Wells-next-the-Sea Urban District
Council* [1973] Ch. 110; and *Sovmots Investments* v. *Secretary of State for the
Environment* [1977] Q.B. 411; [1979] A.C. 144.
[27] *Supra*, at p. 22.
[28] [1971] 1 W.L.R. 204. See also the comment by J. M. Evans in (1972) 35 M.L.R.
88.

Brandrose. In *Dowty Boulton Paul* a local authority had granted
a company certain rights over a municipal airfield. During the
currency of the agreement the authority decided to develop the
airfield as a housing estate. It was argued for the authority that
they could not fetter the exercise of their housing powers and that
they were therefore entitled to override the agreement.

Pennycuick V.C. took the view that the original agreement was
a valid exercise of statutory powers. "Obviously," he said, "where
a power is exercised in such a manner as to create a right extending
over a term of years, the existence of that right *pro tanto* excludes
the exercise of other statutory powers in respect of the same
subject matter."[29] While he accepted that the *Ayr* and *York*
decisions established that a body entrusted with statutory powers
cannot by contract fetter the exercise of those powers, Pennycuick
V.C. thought that that principle was "wholly inapplicable" in the
circumstances of the case before him. The *Ayr* and *York* cases
were, he said "concerned with attempts to fetter in advance the
future exercise of statutory powers otherwise than by the valid
exercise of a statutory power. The cases are not concerned with
the position which arises after a statutory power has been validly
exercised." In the case before him the authority had made an
agreement under statutory powers which excluded the exercise of
other statutory powers in respect of that land; but, he said: "there
is no authority and I can see no principle on which that sort of
exercise could be held to be invalid as a fetter on the future
exercise of powers." To some extent Sir John Pennycuick may be
playing with words, presumably to enable him to distinguish the
leading cases he mentions, but there appears to be force in the
view that the exercise of one statutory power can, in some
circumstances at least, validly restrict the future exercise of other
powers relating to the same subject.

It is not possible to reconcile all the decisions in this area of the
law but it does seem to us that a contractual restriction on an
authority's power will only be held to be invalid as a renunciation
of their "statutory birthright" if there is clear conflict with the
policy of the empowering legislation or if it is clear that one power
is to take precedence over another.[30] We would tentatively suggest
that the real test of a contract's validity is not whether the future
exercise of some statutory power may be restricted by the contract
but rather whether there is a real likelihood[31] that the contract

[29] *Supra*, at p. 210.
[30] See *Blake* v. *Hendon Corporation* (*supra*).
[31] Not a mere possibility—see *British Transport Commission* v. *Westmorland County Council, supra*.

would seriously conflict[32] with some essential function of the contracting authority.[33] In the town planning context, and in the context of section 50, much will also depend on the interpretation of subsection (3).

Brandrose at first instance

The only case in which it has been necessary to consider the question whether a planning authority may legitimately restrict their powers by means of a section 52 agreement is *Windsor & Maidenhead Royal Borough Council* v. *Brandrose Investments*.[34] In this case a planning authority, in accordance with an agreement made under section 52, granted planning permission for the redevelopment of a site. The development necessarily involved the demolition of buildings on the site. Before demolition of these buildings took place, the planning authority decided to extend an existing conservation area in such a way that it included the development site. One effect of the designation of an area as a conservation area is that the consent of the planning authority is required for the demolition of any building in the area. When the developers began to demolish buildings on the development site, the planning authority sought an injunction to restrain them from doing so. The main issue before the court was whether the authority could lawfully enter into an agreement which would operate so as to exclude the exercise of the authority's statutory powers to prevent the demolition of buildings on the site. It was held that an agreement under section 52 could validly fetter such powers. In view of the importance of this decision it appears worthwhile to recount the main points of the judgment.

In argument for the planning authority reference was made to

---

[32] Logically the question ought to be whether there was such a conflict at the time the contract was made, but in the *Westmorland* case there seems to be some suggestion that the test is to be applied at the time the case comes to court.

[33] We would suggest that a test of this kind accords with the decisions of the House of Lords in *Paterson* v. *Provost of St Andrews* (1881) 6 App. Cas. 833; 8 R.(H.L.) 117; *Ayr Harbour Trustees* (as explained in *Birkdale*); and *British Transport Commission* v. *Westmorland County Council* (*supra*). See J. D. B. Mitchell. *The Contracts of Public Authorities*, pp. 57–63; and P. Rogerson, "*On the Fettering of Public Powers*" [1971] P.L. 288. J. F. Garner suggested that it is only when a contract between a public authority and another person may have the effect of restricting the exercise of the authority's discretionary power in relation to a person who is not a party to the contract that there can be an unlawful fetter on the authority's discretion ("The Control of Discretion" (1982) 126 Sol.Jo. 108). This test has attractions but it seems to us that the leading cases show clearly that it cannot represent the present law.

[34] [1981] 1 W.L.R. 1083.

the decision in *Ransom & Luck* (*supra*) and to Lord Greene's comments in that case as to the improbability of Parliament authorising planning authorities to contract out of their statutory duties. Fox J. said that he bore those comments in mind, but it was, he thought, plain that Parliament could by appropriate language authorise authorities to enter into agreements limiting the subsequent exercise of their powers. The question was whether Parliament had done so by section 52.

Fox J. said that it was clear that section 52 was very different in its language from section 34 of the 1932 Act (with which *Ransom & Luck* was concerned). Section 34 dealt only with the case where a landowner was willing to agree to conditions "restricting the planning, development or use of land" whereas section 52 begins with a wide general authority to the planning authority to enter into any agreement for the purpose of "restricting or regulating the development or use" of land.

He thought, however, that the fundamental difference between the two sections was to be found in the provisions of subsection (3) of section 52 (set out *supra*) which had no counterpart in section 34. In Fox J.'s view subsection (3) contemplated the existence, as a result of a section 52 agreement, of fetters upon the powers of a planning authority. With one important exception, a planning authority could, he thought, legitimately restrict the exercise of its powers in relation to the land to which a section 52 agreement related. The exception was where the subsequent exercise of power was in accordance with the development plan or with any direction which might have been given by the Secretary of State as to the provisions to be included in any such plan. Walton J., who had dealt with this case at an earlier stage, reached a similar conclusion as to the effect of subsection (3).

It seemed to Fox J., as it had to Sir John Pennycuick in *Dowty Boulton Paul* (*supra*), that there was "nothing in principle to prevent the exercise of a statutory power being limited by the previous exercise of another statutory power." The exercise of the powers conferred by section 52 could validly limit the power the authority would otherwise have had to prevent demolition of buildings in a conservation area.

Though it seems to us that the meaning given to section 52 by Fox J. is that which Parliament is most likely to have intended, it should perhaps be noted that this reading of the section leans heavily on subsection (3). The subsection is worded in a curiously negative way and can be interpreted in several different ways[35] as

---

[35] See in particular, R. N. D. Hamilton, *Guide to Development and Planning* (7th

is demonstrated by the Court of Appeal's decision in *Brandrose*, a decision which indicates that *Ransom & Luck* has not been laid to rest.[36]

Brandrose in the Court of Appeal

The plaintiffs, Windsor & Maidenhead Royal Borough Council, appealed to the Court of Appeal against Fox J.'s decision.[37] Their appeal was successful but the Court of Appeal's decision was not a satisfactory one for anyone seeking clear guidance as to the meaning of section 52(3).

The Court of Appeal were in the words of Lawton L.J., "unable to construe the difficult subsection (3) as restricting the exercise by a local planning authority of any of their statutory powers which they have a public duty to exercise.[38] It is trite law that a statutory body which has public duties to perform (and a local authority are such a body) cannot lawfully agree not to exercise its powers." The court pointed out that an authority had a duty to designate appropriate parts of their district as conservation areas. The plaintiffs had exercised this duty. The court declared: "Whatever section 52(3) means, and we share the bemusement of counsel for the plaintiffs, it cannot in our judgment be construed as empowering a local planning authority to bind themselves not to exercise the powers given to them by section 277 of the Act [their conservation area powers] which they have a public duty to

---

ed.) pp. 352–354; and J. N. Hawke, "Section 52 Agreements and the Fettering of Planning Powers" [1980] J.P.L. 386.

[36] Whereas Fox J. sees subs. (3) as throwing light on the general powers conferred by s. 52, it might be argued that subs. (1) (containing the general powers to enter agreements) is not wide enough to permit a planning authority to fetter its powers and that the proviso contained in subs. (3) cannot be employed to enlarge by implication the scope of subs. (1) (see *West Derby Union* v. *Metropolitan Life Assurance Society* [1897] A.C. 647, *per* Lord Watson at p. 652). As Hamilton suggests, subs. (3) could simply be read as "something inserted *ex abundanti cautela* to preserve the development plan and which does not detract from the general principle laid down by the courts" (*Guide to Development and Planning* (7th ed.), p. 354). It cannot be argued that subs. (3) was inserted by Parliament as a response to the decision in *Ransom & Luck*: that decision was not made until after the passing of the 1947 Act (which contained the predecessor of s. 52).

[37] [1983] 1 W.L.R. 509.

[38] However, the judgment contains the rather odd statement that so long as the planning authority were satisfied that the developers "did not intend, after demolishing the existing buildings, to leave an ugly gap in Peascod Street for a long time they could not properly have refused consent to demolish". Why, if the authority could not restrict its powers, did the court think refusal would be improper?

exercise." As Malcolm Grant says,[39] "The Court examined none of the competing interpretations of subsection (3). They chose instead to subordinate it to the common law rule." Grant also says[40] that *Brandrose* "remains an unhappy and unsatisfying decision, in which the Court of Appeal failed to come to grips with the central issues and failed therefore to provide any decisive guidance on the validity of section 52 agreements." In all the circumstances and for the sake of certainty in this area of the law it is a matter for regret that leave to appeal to the House of Lords was refused.

Subsection (3), the complexities of which the Court of Appeal made little attempt to unravel, is in our view the key to whether, and if so the extent to which, authorities are entitled to fetter their powers by way of agreements. Whether or not one agrees with Fox J.'s conclusions at first instance, his judgment refers to authority and seeks to place the subsection in its statutory context. In contrast the Court of Appeal's judgment appears somewhat perfunctory in nature, consisting, as it largely does, of unsupported assertions.

In *Brandrose*[41] Walton J. expressed the view that it was "within certain general limits . . . highly desirable" that a planning authority should be able, by means of an agreement to do "either of two things: first of all contract not to exercise its statutory powers in the future, or secondly, contract as to the manner in which it will exercise its statutory powers in the future." Since we believe that view to be right we think it most unfortunate that the Court of Appeal's decision may mean that there is no scope for contracts of the kind mentioned by Walton J. It is perhaps noteworthy that in *Western Fish Products Ltd.* v. *Penwith District Council*[42] the Court of Appeal were, in another planning case, very reluctant to permit planning authorities' powers to be fettered by estoppel.

While we find it difficult to support the Court of Appeal's judgment in *Brandrose*, one might agree with their decision to the extent that it would be undesirable for a planning authority to be able to commit themselves to grant planning permission if to do so meant that the authority had to ignore their duty to take account of representations and other material considerations.

It seems clear that the Court of Appeal considered that an authority cannot restrict the exercise of positive *duties* imposed

---

[39] "The Planning After Effects of the *Brandrose* Litigation," 1983 L.G.C. 768.
[40] *Ibid.*
[41] [1980] 1 W.L.R. 1083.
[42] (1978) 77 L.G.R. 185.

upon planning authorities by statute. It is not clear, however, whether it was also the court's view that authorities are prohibited from fettering the future exercise of mere powers.[43] It is, of course, the case that duties cannot always be readily distinguished from powers; in the Court of Appeal's judgment in *Brandrose*, for example, there is inherent in the "duty" as to the designation of conservation areas a large area of discretion on the part of the planning authority. But if the Court of Appeal's judgment is read as implying that planning authorities cannot fetter their powers, subsection (3) of section 50 would appear to be virtually redundant.

There seems to be little doubt that the Court of Appeal's decision means that a planning authority can ignore the provisions of a section 50 agreement if these run counter to their development control duties. The planning authority will still be able to offer a planning permission as a *quid pro quo* for the developer entering into an agreement but any undertakings offered by the authority as to the future exercise of their planning functions cannot safely be relied upon.

---

[43] See on this E. Young and J. Rowan-Robinson, "Section 52 Agreements and the Fettering of Powers" [1982] J.P.L. 673 and the texts and articles cited there. Duties are not always easy to distinguish from discretionary powers. In *Southend-on-Sea Corporation* v. *Hodgson (Wickford)* [1962] 1 Q.B. 416, *e.g.* Lord Parker made the point that "in a case of discretion there is a duty under the statute to exercise a free and unhindered discretion."

CHAPTER 7

PROCEDURAL ASPECTS

The mechanics of making a section 50 agreement

A planning authority cannot compel a landowner to enter into a planning agreement. Authorities do, however, have the ability to refuse planning permission for development proposals which they find unacceptable. In order to be allowed to carry out his proposals a developer may be prepared to make such concessions as will render the proposed development acceptable to the planning authority and to enter into an agreement embodying such concessions. It seems clear that almost all planning agreements come about in some such fashion.

In such a situation the planning authority will, of course, wish to avoid granting an unqualified planning permission until the agreement has been concluded; once permission has been granted there may well be little incentive for the developer to enter into an agreement. Where the planning authority are disposed to grant planning permission if an agreement can be concluded, there are various ways in which they can proceed. Practice varies quite considerably in Scotland.

Some Scottish authorities adopt the simple expedient of not determining the planning application until an agreement has been executed by the landowner. To safeguard the developer, the agreement could be made conditional on the grant of planning permission. Indeed, subject to what is said in Chapter 6 *supra*, it would appear to be legitimate for a planning authority to undertake in the agreement to grant planning permission. However, completion of the agreement in advance of the planning permission can create a problem where the applicant does not yet have an interest in the land (and is therefore unable to make an agreement which binds the land).

The procedure which appears to be most common among Scottish planning authorities is for the authority to determine the application but not to issue the decision notice until the agreement has been executed. A similar approach has been adopted, on occasion, by reporters on appeal.[1] This approach assumes that

---

[1] See, *e.g.* SPADS Nos. A3252, A5461, A5667 and A5639.

there can as a matter of law be no planning permission unless and until written notice of the planning authority's decision has been issued to the applicant. This would seem to be borne out by the decision of Wolfe J. in *R. v. West Oxfordshire District Council, ex p. Pearce Homes Ltd.*[2] Authorities have, it seems, sometimes been prepared, if the developer gives an undertaking to execute the agreement, to issue planning permission in advance of the agreement being executed.

A few Scottish planning authorities grant planning permission subject to a condition requiring the developer to enter into a section 50 agreement.[3] Doubts have been expressed about the propriety of this. In one Scottish planning appeal decision, for example, the reporter expressed the view that "it would not be right to try to give planning permission subject to a condition that an agreement under section 50 be entered into. An attempt to do so might be of doubtful validity."[4] Some support for the reporter's view can be drawn from Woolf J.'s judgment in *McLaren v. Secretary of State for the Environment.*[5]

In this case Woolf J. said that where the Secretary of State, on appeal, considered that an agreement between the planning authority and the developer would be appropriate, it would be open to him before he gave a final decision, to intimate to the planning authority and the appellant that while not requiring it to be done and having no power to compel it to be done, if a section 52 agreement were to be entered into he would regard the case as one where planning permission could be granted. The matter could then be adjourned for a reasonable time to see whether an agreement could be concluded. The Secretary of State would then have the advantage of knowing the position before he came to his decision and could make his decision in that light.

---

[2] [1986] J.P.L. 523. See also *Slough Estates v. Slough Borough Council* (No. 2) [1971] A.C. 958, [1969] 2 Ch. 305; *R. v. Yeovil Borough Council, ex p. Trustees of Elim Pentecostal Church* (1971) 23 P. & C.R. 39; and *Co-operative Retail Services v. Taff-Ely Borough Council* (1978) 38 P. & C.R. 156 (overruled on other grounds by the Court of Appeal). See also (1974) 37 M.L.R. 338; [1975] J.P.L. 682; and [1976] J.P.L. 101. Note also the Local Government and Planning (Scotland) Act 1982, Sched. 2, and paras. 8 and 16 which provide that the date of the decision will be the date which the decision notice bears.
[3] See also the decision by the Secretary of State for Scotland reported at [1981] J.P.L. 301. See also SPADS No. A5639.
[4] SPADS A3252. See also the appeal decision noted at [1980] J.P.L. 841. The decision letter on that appeal went on to state, however, that the Secretary of State accepted that "it is open to a planning authority to refuse permission if satisfactory arrangements have not been concluded for the timely provision of essential physical or, in exceptional cases, social infrastructure."
[5] [1981] J.P.L. 423.

We find it difficult to see what objection there could be to a condition which required an agreement to be entered into dealing with matters which are within the normal scope of planning conditions and which may, in fact, be the subject of conditions in the planning permission. The fact that there is a condition on the permission dealing with such matters does not render the agreement entirely superfluous. It would provide the planning authority with an alternative means of enforcement—a sort of belt and braces situation. The agreement, unlike the condition, could also provide for direct action by the planning authority in the event of default. However, it seems to us that in order to be enforceable, such a condition would have to specify all the terms of the proposed agreement or, at the very least, refer to heads of agreement. This difficulty was recognised by a reporter in one appeal.[6] The reporter was minded to grant planning permission subject to a condition that a section 50 agreement be entered into. He considered, however, that this might cause problems. The terms of any such agreement were not known, even in outline, and he feared that permission subject to such a condition lacked adequate specification. Therefore, instead of granting a conditional planning permission, he considered the proper course was to use his letter as an interim decision, allowing the parties to adjust matters of detail and to draft and execute an appropriate agreement. (The section 50 agreement was to be used to resolve drainage problems and also to safeguard trees.) The reporter stated that he would be prepared to issue planning permission finally when the agreement had been made. From the point of view of the planning authority, a condition requiring an agreement to be entered into would seem to have the disadvantage that it would be open to the applicant to appeal to the Secretary of State against the condition and the condition might be discharged on appeal.

Conversely, it seems to us that where a proposed agreement is to include matters which are beyond the scope of planning conditions, for example, a requirement that the developer should reimburse the cost to the local authority of providing public services, then a condition on a grant of planning permission which required such an obligation to be undertaken by a developer would be *ultra vires*.

This view appears to coincide with that of the Scottish Development Department. In SDD Circular 18/1986, the Department assert, in the context of conditions requiring the payment of money or other consideration for the grant of permission, "[s]imilarly,

---

[6] SPADS No. A5667.

permission should not be granted subject to a condition that the applicant enters into an agreement under Section 50 of the Act or other powers."[7]

Some Scottish authorities have adopted the practice of granting planning permission subject to what amounts to a suspensive condition—the permission provides that it is not to be effective until an agreement (on terms which have already been negotiated) is concluded. Some authorities go rather further and lay down that the planning permission is not to become effective until the agreement has been recorded in the Register of Sasines.[8]

In the case of other planning authorities the normal practice is for the authority to indicate to the applicant its approval in principle of the application and to delegate to the appropriate officials power to grant planning permission once a section 50 agreement covering specified matters has been concluded.[9] Execution of the agreement and the grant of planning permission can then take place simultaneously.

There is, of course nothing to prevent the planning agreement itself being used as the document which grants planning permission. This would seem to have the disadvantage that the agreement would have to include the reasons for the imposition of any conditions and would have to contain notification of the applicant's rights of appeal. At least two Scottish planning authorities have, however, taken the course of including the decision notice as a Schedule to the agreement.

Where an applicant does not currently have an interest capable of binding the land, SDD Circular 22/1984 suggests that a planning authority should consider giving the applicant an *indication* that planning permission will be forthcoming if a section 50 agreement is eventually duly recorded or registered. This would enable the applicant to complete title and, thereafter, to enter into the agreement. Planning permission could then be issued. An alternative approach favoured by some authorities and applicants is to complete an agreement under section 69 of the Local Government (Scotland) Act 1973 whereby the applicant undertakes upon

---

[7] Para 69. See also DoE Circular 1/85, para. 63.

[8] In an appeal relating to large scale residential development in the green belt, a reporter stated that it was a requirement of his decision that agreements under s. 50 of the 1972 Act and s. 69 of the 1973 Act be executed and (where appropriate) duly recorded prior to implementation and he imposed a condition that the permission would not take effect until that had been done. (P/PPA/GA/160, July 18, 1984).

[9] This was the approach contemplated by the planning authorities in the *West Oxfordshire D.C.* and *Yeovil* cases (*supra*).

infeftment to complete a section 50 agreement in defined terms. Planning permission is issued upon completion of the section 69 agreement. Caution needs to be exercised by authorities in such cases to cover the position of some person other than the applicant becoming infeft of the land and implementing the permission.

In their response to our questionnaires, planning authorities drew attention to certain difficulties encountered in negotiating agreements with developers and their agents. Several authorities referred to difficulties encountered by applicants (who had not yet acquired title) in persuading landowners to sign agreements. Similar problems had arisen in a number of cases with respect to heritable creditors. Perhaps the most common complaint was about the length of time which sometimes elapsed before a planning permission could be issued. This was attributed variously to difficulties in mobilising the authority's legal section, in establishing title, in obtaining signatures and in recording agreements. In some cases developers apparently decided not to proceed with their proposals when they were informed that the planning authority would require them to enter into an agreement, in one case because of an inability to obtain mortgage finance. On the other hand, one or two respondents made the point that developers and their advisers sometimes did not appear to appreciate the potential strength of their negotiating position; this was attributed to lack of knowledge of planning law and procedures.

Mention should perhaps be made here of the decision in *Augier* v. *Secretary of State for the Environment*[10] which arose out of the inability of developers to enter into an agreement under section 52 of the Town and Country Planning Act 1971. At a public inquiry into an appeal against refusal of planning permission, the applicants attempted to meet certain objections to their proposals by offering to provide visibility splays at the end of the road giving access to their proposed development. They did not, however, own the land necessary to provide adequate sight lines. It was their hope that they would be able (presumably through an arrangement with the owner of the land) to enter into a section 52 agreement relating to the visibility splays. No such agreement had been concluded by the time the appeal came to be decided, but the Secretary of State declared that he was satisfied that the developers would be able to provide adequate sight lines. He therefore granted planning permission subject to a condition that the developers were to provide visibility splays in accordance with

---

[10] (1978) 38 P. & C.R. 219 (reported *sub nom. Hildenborough Village Preservation Association* v. *Secretary of State for the Environment* [1978] J.P.L. 708).

a scheme to be approved by the local planning authority. The validity of that decision was challenged.

Sir Douglas Frank held that where an applicant for planning permission gave an undertaking and, relying on that undertaking, the planning authority or the Secretary of State granted planning permission subject to a condition the terms of which were broad enough to embrace the undertaking, the applicant could not later be heard to say that there was no power to require compliance with the undertaking.[11] In such circumstances the applicant would be barred from going back on his undertaking. In Sir Douglas Frank's view this conclusion was not only in accordance with commonsense, it meant that the parties were able to avoid the formality, expense and delay involved in an agreement under section 52 of the 1971 Act.

It seems to us that a planning authority would be unwise to rely on such an undertaking. Whatever its legal effect as regards the person who gave it, it does not seem that the undertaking would be binding upon successors in title. Even against the party who gave it, it is not clear how such an undertaking is to be enforced.

Recording of agreements

Section 50(2) provides that an agreement will be enforceable at the instance of the planning authority against persons deriving title from the person with whom the agreement was made, provided the agreement is recorded in the appropriate Register of Sasines. The effect of this subsection has already been considered.[12]

Research by Cramond and Bruce[13] showed that some 70 section 50 agreements were entered into in Scotland between 1969 and 1978. The *Practice Note on Section 50 Agreements* published in 1981 by the Scottish Branch of the RICS[14] stated that the Department of the Registers of Scotland had "indicated that on average only one or two planning agreements per year have been recorded since the 1972 Act came into force with the preponderance of these coming from one particular area." This would seem to indicate that many agreements were not recorded. We think it very likely (though we have been unable to make a complete

---

[11] This would now seem doubtful given the Court of Appeal's decision in *City of Bradford Metropolitan Council* v. *Secretary of State for the Environment and McLean Homes Northern Ltd* [1986] J.P.L. 598, to the effect that an unreasonable condition does not become reasonable simply because an applicant consents to its terms.

[12] See Chaps. 1 and 2 *supra*.

[13] See App. 3 (bibliography).

[14] See App. 3 (bibliography).

check) that the *Practice Note* is mistaken. Almost all of the section 50 agreements that we have seen have been recorded. With two exceptions, all of the authorities who responded to our questionnaires stated that all the section 50 agreements they have made either had been or were in the process of being recorded. Of the exceptions, one authority informed us that two of their 16 completed agreements had not been recorded. Both agreements had been made with a firm of housebuilders who were apparently somewhat reluctant to see the agreements recorded because they envisaged minor problems in connection with the sale of their houses. The planning authority had agreed not to record the agreements—in one case because there were doubts about the enforceability of the agreement and in the other case because the agreement required only a single act on the part of the developers and it was clear that the agreement would in fact be implemented. The other authority had experienced difficulty in drafting their agreements in a style acceptable to the Registrar for incorporation in the Register of Sasines.

Delay in the recording of an agreement might give rise to problems; the proviso to section 50(2) means that an agreement cannot be enforced against a third party who has, in good faith and for value, acquired right to the land prior to the recording of the agreement. One planning authority informed us of a problem of this kind caused by delay in the recording of a section 50 agreement resulting from the civil servants' strike in 1981. As that authority suggested, this sort of problem might be avoided by including in the agreement a provision to the effect that the land was not to be disposed of to a third party until the agreement had been recorded. We have seen a few agreements which provide that the benefit of the *planning permission* is not to be transferred until the agreement has been recorded.

Variation and termination of section 50 agreements

Section 50(1) states that an agreement may be entered into for the purpose of restricting or regulating the development or use of land, "either permanently or during such period as may be prescribed by the agreement."

The agreement itself may provide for its coming to an end— perhaps at the end of a prescribed period or after the carrying out of specified works. It may, by implication, come to an end after the carrying out of prescribed works. Several of the Scottish agreements we have seen provide that when the works required by the agreement have been carried out, the planning authority will grant a formal discharge.

An agreement may become obsolete with the passage of time or as a result of changes in planning policy. Changed circumstances may also result in an agreement having unforeseen or undesirable consequences. Where an agreement has outlived its usefulness or its terms require modification, the parties can agree that the agreement should be brought to an end or its terms varied. In some cases specific provision is made for the termination of the agreement by mutual written agreement of the parties. Specific provision of this kind would not appear to be necessary. In *Hope* v. *Secretary of State for the Environment*[15] an inspector appointed to determine a planning appeal dismissed the appeal, his decision being based in part on the belief that two agreements which the appellants had offered to enter into under section 52 of the Town and Country Planning Act 1971 would sterilise the land for the purposes of future development. It was held by Phillips J. that the inspector had erred in law; if the planning authority changed its policy it could always release the other party to the agreement. One agreement we have seen provides that its terms may be varied from time to time by agreement; in the event of failure to agree, any question of variation of the section 50 agreement is to be remitted for decision to a man of skill appointed by the sheriff, the decision to be binding upon the parties.

Many agreements relate, even if indirectly, to a grant of planning permission. Revocation or modification of that permission would have no effect upon the agreement, even though its terms might then be rendered inappropriate. In one case, an appellant sought to argue that a section 50 agreement had no effect independently of the planning permission to which it was related.[16] The agreement would fall, it was contended, if a fresh planning permission was granted in respect of the land. That argument failed. Once recorded or registered, it is clear from the terms of section 50 that an agreement will run with the land. Thus, even though the agreement may have been triggered by an application for planning permission, it will, unless contrary provision is made in the agreement, operate independently of the permission and may be enforceable even though the permission has not been implemented or, alternatively, may remain in force after the development which was the subject of the permission has ceased. It may be that provision should sometimes be made in the agreement for variation of its terms in the event of the planning permission being revoked or modified. And a number of the agreements we have seen provide that if the

---

[15] (1975) 31 P. & C.R. 120.
[16] SPADS No. A5064 (reported at (1985) 14 S.P.L.P. 28).

development is not proceeded with or is abandoned or if the land in question ceases to be used for the purposes of the development to which the agreement relates, then the agreement is to be null and void and the authority are to grant a discharge of the obligations contained in the agreement.

In England and Wales the Lands Tribunal is empowered, on the application of any person interested in freehold land affected by a restriction arising under a covenant, to vary or discharge any such restrictions.[17] It is clear that application may be made for the variation of discharge of a covenant contained in an agreement made under section 52 of the Town and Country Planning Act 1971.[18] The Lands Tribunal for Scotland has a comparable though not identical, jurisdiction under section 1 of the Conveyancing and Feudal Reform (Scotland) Act 1970 to vary or discharge land obligations if the Tribunal is satisfied that the obligation in question has become unreasonable or inappropriate as a result of changes in the character of the land or the neighbourhood, or is unduly burdensome compared with any benefit resulting from it, or impedes some reasonable use of land. Several of those who responded to our earlier questionnaire suggested that a landowner would be entitled to make application to the Lands Tribunal for Scotland under section 1 of the 1970 Act for variation or discharge of any obligations contained in a section 50 agreement.[19]

We have very considerable doubts as to whether such an application is competent. Section 1 of the 1970 Act is concerned with the variation and discharge of "land obligations." A land obligation is "an obligation relating to land which is enforceable by a proprietor of an interest in land by virtue of his being such proprietor, and which is binding upon a proprietor of another interest in that land, or of an interest in other land, by virtue of his being such proprietor."[20] Interest in land means "any estate or interest in land which is capable of being owned or held as a

---

[17] Law of Property Act 1925, s. 84.
[18] See *Gee* v. *National Trust* [1966] 1 W.L.R. 170; *Re Beecham Group Ltd.'s Application* (1980) 256 E.G. 829; [1981] J.P.L. 55; *Re Bovis Homes Southern Ltd.'s Application* [1981] J.P.L. 368; *Re Cox's Application* [1985] J.P.L. 564; *Re Martin's Application* (1986) 53 P. & C.R. 146; *Re Kentwood Properties Ltd.'s Application* [1987] J.P.L. 137; and *Abbey Homesteads (Developments) Ltd* v. *Northamptonshire County Council et. al.* [1986] J.P.L. 683. See also Anthony J. Ward, "Planning Agreements and the March of Time: Removing Obsolete Restrictions" [1981] J.P.L. 557, and Barry Denyer-Green, "Planning Agreements: Discharge or Modification of Restrictive Covenants" (1988) 8807 E.G. 63.
[19] See also RICS *Practice Note*, p. 11.
[20] Conveyancing and Feudal Reform Act 1970, s. 1(2).

separate interest and to which a title may be recorded in the Register of Sasines."[21] It seems to us that the planning authority are not, by virtue of a section 50 agreement, the proprietors of an interest in land, that an obligation contained in a section 50 agreement is not enforceable by or against the planning authority by virtue of their being proprietor of an interest in land, that an obligation contained in such an agreement is therefore not a land obligation and that the provisions of section 1 of the 1970 Act can in consequence have no application in relation to section 50 agreements.[22]

Ensuring compliance with the terms of an agreement

The response to our recent questionnaire shows that the great majority of Scottish planning authorities monitor agreements to ensure compliance; and it would seem that there is a reasonably high degree of compliance with such agreements. However, on three occasions recently authorities have sought to enforce agreements through the courts. In all three cases a satisfactory remedy was secured without the need to obtain decree. The first case concerned a failure to fulfil an obligation to demolish an existing building upon completion and occupation of a replacement dwelling. In the second an action was raised to secure a reduction in the number of residential caravans on a site to the level stipulated in an agreement. And the third case involved a failure adequately to comply with landscaping provisions in an agreement.

A further instance in which a developer failed in a material way to comply with the terms of an agreement did not result in court action but has achieved some notoriety. It concerned two section 50 agreements which a district planning authority had negotiated with two separate firms of housebuilders. The agreements were designed to govern the rate at which private houses were to be built on a particular site. The agreements reflected the district planning authority's view of what constituted a reasonable rate of growth for the village in question, the region's ability to provide the necessary infrastructure and the requirements of the developers as regards rate of progress. Part of the development site was sold to another housing developer who proceeded to build a number of houses on part of the site in contravention of the terms of the agreements.

---

[21] *Ibid*. s. 2(6).

[22] If we are wrong in this view, and an obligation contained in a s. 50 agreement is a land obligation, it seems clear that the Lands Tribunal would have jurisdiction to vary or discharge the obligation, even though it is imposed under statutory powers—see *Mrs Ann Munro Macdonald Applicant* 1973 S.L.T. (Lands Tr.) 26.

Thirty-two of these houses were completed and sold-off. One might have expected that the solicitors acting for the purchasers of the houses would have raised some question about compliance with the agreements (which had been recorded), but apparently none did so.[23] The planning authority agreed, after negotiation, to an amendment of the terms of the agreement so as to allow the 32 houses to remain. In a situation of this kind it may be that a planning authority has little option but to agree to amendment. However, the authority refused to give way on other, uncompleted, houses which the developer had built in contravention of the agreements.

It seems clear that many local authority officers see it as a major benefit of section 50 agreements that the parties to an agreement have available to them the various remedies provided by the ordinary law of contract. In particular, the parties will be able to take action in the courts to ensure compliance with the terms of the agreement. As Fox L.J. observed in *Avon County Council* v. *Millard and Another*[24] of the corresponding provision in the English Planning Act of 1971 "Parliament, by section 52, gave power to local authorities to enter into such a contract as this. There is nothing in section 52 which indicates that ordinary civil remedies for breach of such contract were not to be available." The Court of Appeal in that case granted an interlocutory injunction to restrain mineral operations being carried on in contravention of a provision in a section 52 agreement.

In addition, an agreement may specify alternative or additional steps that may be taken to secure compliance with, or to provide remedies for breach of, the terms of the agreement. Various provisions of this kind are to be found in the agreements we have seen. What is appropriate for a particular agreement will, of course, depend to a very great degree on the nature of the matters regulated by that agreement.

Agreements requiring a developer to carry out works on land sometimes confer default powers upon the planning authority. Some such agreements provide that in the event of the developer failing to carry out his obligations, the authority are to be entitled

---

[23] As was said in the *Journal of the Law Society of Scotland*: "It is . . . important for the solicitor for the purchaser of a new house (whether or not missives have been cpmpleted and whether or not the builder is under obligation to produce planning permissions or searches) to ascertain whether or not a section 50 agreement is in existence, and if so, what its terms are and whether they have been complied with by the builder" (1981) 26 J.L.S. 464).

[24] (1985) 274 E.G. 1025. And see *Abbey Homesteads (Developments) Ltd.* v. *Northamptonshire County Council et al.* [1986] J.P.L. 683.

to carry out the works or to take whatever other action is required of the developer by the agreement, and to recover their costs from the developer.[25] A number of agreements we have seen provide that if the developers fail to comply with an order of the planning authority requiring them to take steps to remedy any significant or continued breach of the agreements, the planning authority are to be entitled to rescind the relevant planning permission without compensation or to suspend the permission until the developers have remedied the breach. The agreements go on to provide that in the event of such rescission the developers are to terminate the development and to cease using the premises for the purposes envisaged by the agreements, all without any right to compensation. Some of these agreements declare that it is for the planning authority alone to determine what constitutes a "significant" or "continued" breach of the agreement.

It is fairly common to provide that, without prejudice to the other remedies that may be available to the planning authority, a breach of agreement is to be deemed a breach of planning control entitling the authority to serve an enforcement notice under section 84 of the 1972 Act. It seems to us that before a provision of this kind would enable a planning authority to serve an enforcement notice in respect of some act that is not a breach of planning control as defined in section 84(2) of the 1972 Act, the terms of the agreement will have to have been incorporated as conditions or limitations on the planning permission.

Some agreements contain provisions designed to ensure that if the developer defaults on his obligations under the agreement or goes into liquidation, there will be paid to the planning authority a sum intended to cover the cost of carrying out works required by the agreement or any loss sustained by the authority as a result of the developer's failure. Financial provisions of this kind are, as one would expect, most commonly found in agreements relating to such developments as quarrying, opencast mining and pipelaying—cases where the planning authority will be concerned to find a way of ensuring that after the carrying out of the development, conditions as to restoration works are complied with. In most such cases payment is guaranteed by a bank or insurance company.

---

[25] Scottish authorities do not possess such powers under an agreement unless specific provision to that effect is embodied in the agreement. In England and Wales, however, s. 33 of the Local Government (Miscellaneous Provisions) Act 1982 provides that an authority may, on giving 21 days notice, enter on land and carry out work or do any other thing required by a covenant to which the section applies and to recover the cost from any person against whom the covenant is enforceable.

It is fairly common for agreements to provide that officials of
the planning authority are to have the right to enter on the land
to which the agreement relates in order to satisfy themselves
that the agreement is being complied with. Rights of entry are
sometimes conferred for other purposes—for example, to enable
the authority to carry out works required by the agreement.

Drafting and interpretation of agreements

Planning agreements can be difficult to draft. As was pointed
out by one of those who responded to our questionnaires, a section
50 agreement is likely to relate to future development and the
requirements of the agreement can therefore be difficult to state
in language sufficiently precise to enable successful court action to
be taken in the event of breach. We think this an important point.
The need for careful drafting is well illustrated by two decisions
of the English courts.

In *National Trust* v. *Midlands Electricity Board*[26] a deed granted
in favour of the National Trust declared that "No act or thing shall
be done or placed or permitted to remain upon the land which
shall injure, prejudice, affect or destroy the natural aspect and
condition of the land." Vaisey J. thought the wording of this
restriction "extremely inapt and ill-considered." It would, he said,
"be difficult to find wider, vaguer and more indeterminate words
than these." The restriction was held void for uncertainty.

However, it is interesting to contrast this decision with that in
United Bill Posting Co. Ltd. v. *Somerset County Council.*[27] A bye-
law which provided that no advertisements were to be exhibited
so as to disfigure the natural beauty of the landscape was challenged
on the ground of uncertainty. The court dismissed the challenge.
Natural beauty was not a thing which could be defined by specific
instances. The appellants were asking the local authority to define
the indefinable. Of the two decisions, that in the *Midlands
Electricity Board* is likely to be more relevant in the context of
section 50 agreements, concerned as it was with the amenity of an
identifiable parcel of land.

In *Crittenden (Warren Park) Ltd.* v. *Surrey County Council*[28] an
agreement under section 25 of the Town and Country Planning
Act 1947 restricted to 25 the number of caravans to be stationed
on a particular site. However, the agreement also contained a
provision preserving the landowner's rights under the Town and

---

[26] [1952] Ch. 380.
[27] (1926) 42 T.L.R. 537.
[28] [1966] 1 W.L.R. 25.

Country Planning Acts. It was held that this provision preserved not only the owner's compensation rights but also any existing use rights attaching to the site. On the facts it was found that these included the right to station caravans on the site and the court took the view that the latter rights overrode the limitation on numbers contained in the agreement. As a result the landowner was held entitled to have 33 caravans on the site.

A further illustration of the importance of careful drafting is provided by the report of an appeal decision.[29] During the course of the appeal the planning authority sought to argue that the appeal site was already subject to restrictions concerning the type of goods to be sold imposed by a section 50 agreement linked to an earlier planning permission. The agreement did not specify the area to which its terms applied and the reporter considered that being a contract creating land conditions the agreement had to be construed strictly. The preamble in the agreement did narrate that the appellant owned the whole four acre site but it did not provide that the agreement affected the whole area. That being so, the scope of the restrictions effected by the agreement had to be deduced from the clauses specifying them. Thus, for example, a clause stating that only horticultural goods might be sold from the garden centre applied only to the garden centre part of the site.

In Scotland the courts have tended to interpret contracts relating to land fairly strictly.[30] We suspect that they would be likely to interpret a section 50 agreement more narrowly than an ordinary commercial contract.

It is not clear whether one could competently look at the terms of any related planning permission in order to resolve any ambiguity in a section 50 agreement.[31]

Some of the agreements we have seen provide for the reference of disputes on the interpretation of the agreement to the Secretary of State or to a person appointed by him or by the sheriff, the decision to be final and binding on the parties.

Public involvement
While there may well be an opportunity for public comment on

---

[29] SPADS No. A5064. See also *Abbey Homesteads (Developments) Ltd.* v. *Northamptonshire County Council et al.* [1986] J.P.L. 683.
[30] See Rankine, *The Law of Landownership in Scotland* (4th ed.), pp. 482–487; Burns, *Conveyancing Practice* (4th ed.), p. 226; Walker, *The Law of Contracts and Related Obligations in Scotland* (2nd ed.), para. 8.10.; McBryde, *The Law of Contract in Scotland* (1987), Chap. 19.
[31] See *L.A.H. Ames Ltd.* v. *North Bedfordshire Borough Council* [1980] J.P.L. 182, (1979) 253 E.G. 55, and *Abbey Homesteads (Developments) Ltd.* v. *Northamptonshire County Council et al.* [1986] J.P.L. 683.

a planning application which gives rise to a section 50 agreement, there is no statutory provision for public involvement in matters which are the subject of negotiations relating to an agreement. This has sometimes been the subject of criticism and of proposals for change.[32] The response to our questionnaires shows that, with one or two exceptions, planning authorities do not go out of their way to invite comments from the public on such matters. As is mentioned above, however, section 50(3) provides a degree of protection for the development plan, in the making of which members of the public will have had opportunities to be involved.[33]

The terms of a planning agreement do not have to be entered in the register of planning applications kept by the planning authority. Once an agreement has been recorded in the Register of Sasines a member of the public could, with some difficulty, ascertain the terms of the agreement, but it is, perhaps, a pity that section 50 agreements were not included in the list of matters which planning authorities are required to enter in a public register as a result of section 44 of the Local Government and Planning (Scotland) Act 1982.

---

[32] See, e.g. Jeffrey Jowell, "Bargaining in Development Control" [1977] J.P.L. 414; Jeffrey Jowell, "The Limits of the Law in Urban Planning" [1977] C.L.P. 63; Roger W. Suddards, "Section 52 Agreements: A Case for New Legislation" [1979] J.P.L. 661; and Martin Loughlin, "Planning Gain: Law, Policy and Practice" (1981) 1 Oxford Jo. of Legal Studies 61; Ian Simpson, "Planning Gain: An Aid to Positive Planning?" in M. L. Harrison and R. Mordey (eds.), *Planning Control: Philosophies, Prospects and Practice* (Croom Helm, 1987), chap. 6.
[33] See Chap. 6 *supra*.

CHAPTER 8

THE USE OF AGREEMENTS IN SCOTLAND

Introduction

THE information about the use that has been made of agreements in Scotland contained in this chapter is based on the response to two questionnaires which we circulated to planning authorities in 1982 and 1987. In 1982 we sent out a questionnaire together with an accompanying letter to all general and district planning authorities. Four of the six general planning authorities and 21 of the 37 district planning authorities responded—a response rate of 58 per cent. In 1987 we repeated the exercise, including regional planning authorities on this occasion following clarification of their ability to enter into such agreements.[1] We received responses to the second questionnaire from all six general planning authorities, from 32 of the 37 district planning authorities and from three of the six regional planning authorities—a response rate of 84 per cent.

In a number of instances, responses were followed up by letter, telephone or interview. Some discussion has taken place by telephone with a number of authorities who did not respond to the questionnaire. In addition, we have had access to the results of research into the use of section 50 agreements carried out by two students in 1978.[2] Many authorities also provided us with photocopies of agreements and we have seen well over a hundred of these.

The two questionnaire surveys between them encompass the period commencing with the re-organisation of local government in Scotland in May 1975. The extent to which agreements were used prior to that date is uncertain. Bruce states that up to 1969, when the requirement to obtain the Secretary of State's consent was repealed, only six agreements had been completed in the

---

[1] s. 50(4) of the 1972 Act, added by Local Government and Planning (Scotland) Act 1982, Sched. 2, para. 14.

[2] J. Douglas Cramond, "Planning by Agreement" (thesis submitted for degree of B.Sc., Heriot-Watt University, 1979); Isabel Bruce, "Section 50 Agreements and Enforcement" (thesis submitted for Diploma in Town Planning, University of Strathclyde, 1979).

whole of Scotland.[3] It is probable that rather more were completed between 1969 and the re-organisation of local government in 1975.

There is no means of knowing how many planning agreements are currently in operation as some agreements are of limited duration. However, we are in a position to say something about the extent to which these agreements are being employed by planning authorities. The response to our 1982 questionnaire showed that 165 agreements had been completed since May 1975. The response to our 1987 questionnaire showed that in the five years from 1982 a further 496 agreements had been completed. This indicates a very considerable increase in the use being made of agreements. Inevitably, the figures show considerable variation between authorities but 27 authorities acknowledged some increase or a substantial increase in their use of agreements. Thirteen authorities had concluded more than 20 agreements over this period; and of these, six had concluded more than 30 agreements. Eleven had concluded 5 or less. Only four authorities stated they had made no use of agreements.

Overall the picture which has emerged is one of growing interest on the part of authorities in Scotland in planning by agreement.

Agreements in practice

Section 50 agreements may fall into one or more of four categories:[4]
1. Agreements restricting the development of land.
2. Agreements regulating the development of land.
3. Agreements restricting the use of land.
4. Agreements regulating the use of land.

To illustrate the use which has been made of section 50 agreements in Scotland we have attempted to group them into these four categories. Some agreements deal with a range of matters and therefore appear in more than one category. In view of the uncertainty about the dividing line between agreements which "restrict" and agreements which "regulate", the grouping may at times seem a little arbitrary.

1. Agreements restricting the development of land

Grouped within this category are those cases where development has been, or is to be, granted planning permission subject to some prohibition or restriction.

The most obvious example is the case where an agreement

---

[3] Isabel Bruce, "Section 50 Agreements and Enforcement," *supra.*
[4] See s. 50(1).

provides that the authorised activity is not to take place on specified land. For example, in three cases agreements associated with the construction of landfall sections of North Sea gas pipelines prohibited the storage of spoil, materials, machinery or equipment on certain land and one of these also prohibited the carrying out of building or engineering operations on the land. In several cases associated with a grant of planning permission for mineral workings, excavation or dumping of spoil is proscribed on identified areas. Such restrictions may also appear as conditions attached to the related planning permission but incorporation into an agreement gives the planning authority greater flexibility as regards enforcement and also avoids the prospect of the restriction being overturned on appeal to the Secretary of State.

It is questionable how far a planning authority may go in prohibiting any further development of specified land by way of a planning condition. A planning authority must determine every application which comes before it and an authority which predetermined an application by way of a condition on an earlier planning permission could be held to be fettering the exercise of discretion.[5] Some authorities appear to take the view that use of a section 50 agreement gets round this uncertainty. In connection with the grant of planning permission, for example for a new dwelling in the grounds of an existing dwelling, an agreement might be entered into restricting any further development of the grounds. We have seen several such agreements.

A rather different type of restriction and one which might well be regarded by the courts as an undue interference with property rights by planning authorities if it appeared as a condition, is a restriction on the alienation of land.[6] We have come across a large number of cases where planning permission for a house has been accompanied by an agreement prohibiting the disposal of the house separately from the economic unit with which it is linked. New houses have been tied in this way to farms, small industrial units, market gardens, fish farms, hotels, a calf-rearing shed, a commercial stable, a restaurant, a caravan site, a chalet park, and a rural post office. In similar fashion "granny flats" have been tied

---

[5] *Stringer* v. *Minister of Housing and Local Government* [1970] 1 W.L.R. 1281. Wade states: "It is a fundamental rule for the exercise of discretionary power that discretion must be brought to bear on every case: each one must be considered on its own merits and decided as the public interest requires at the time." (*Administrative Law* (6th ed., 1988), pp. 370–372). See also Chap. 5.

[6] See also SDD Circular 18/1986, para. 36 which states that as a matter of policy "a condition which would put a severe limitation on the freedom of an owner to dispose of his property, or which would obviously make it difficult to finance the erection of the permitted building by borrowing on mortgage, should be avoided on these grounds."

to houses and a farm shop has been tied to a farm. We have also come across a few cases where planning permission for chalet development has been linked to an agreement prohibiting the disposal of chalets otherwise than as one complete unit.

A further restriction, and one which would seem to fall within the proper scope of a condition, is a limitation on the type of goods which may be sold from commercial premises. Although a change of use within the same use class does not constitute "development" within the meaning of section 19 of the 1972 Act,[7] there is authority to support the view that such a change—for example, from one type of shop to another may be controlled by condition.[8] Nonetheless, we have seen a number of agreements controlling the type of goods to be sold from retail premises. In similar fashion agreements have been employed to prohibit the sale of draught beer from wine bars, to restrict the type of boats using a marina, to restrict the type of goods sold by a builders' merchant, by a factory shop, by a market garden, and by farm shops. We have also been told of agreements containing similar restrictions designed to prevent the loss of service shops to communities. A somewhat similar restriction on use, and one which has formed the subject of a number of agreements, is that which limits the use of chalet development to holidays only.

It is only a short step from an agreement which restricts the use of premises to one which limits the types of person who may occupy premises. Planning control is concerned primarily with the use of land rather than with the user.[9] Nonetheless, provided that underlying a restriction on user there are sound planning considerations relating to use, it would seem that such a restriction may properly be the subject of a condition.[10] However, as a matter of policy, the SDD have taken the view that such conditions should only be employed in fairly narrowly defined circumstances.[11] To

---

[7] See s. 19(2)(f) of the 1972 Act and art. 3(1) of and the Schedule to the Town and Country Planning (Use Classes) (Scotland) Order 1973.

[8] *City of London Corporation* v. *Secretary of State for the Environment* (1972) 23 P. & C.R. 169. SDD Circular 18/1986, however, observes that, as the Use Classes Order is designed to give or confirm a freedom from detailed control, there will be a general presumption against limiting its application in a particular case and that such a condition will require special justification (see paras. 72–77).

[9] See, *Westminster City Council* v. *Great Portland Estates plc* [1984] 3 W.L.R. 1035; and *Westminster City Council* v. *British Waterways Board* [1984] 3 W.L.R. 1047.

[10] *Westminster City Council* v. *Great Portland Estate plc, cit. supra*; and *Fawcett Properties Ltd.* v. *Buckingham County Council* [1961] A.C. 636. But see *David Lowe and Sons Ltd.* v. *Musselburgh Town Council* 1973 S.C. 130; 1974 S.L.T. 5.

[11] See SDD Circular 18/1986, paras. 78–85. And see, generally, the discussion of law and policy in this area in M. Loughlin, *Local Needs, Policies and Development Control Strategies* (School for Advanced Urban Studies Working Paper 42, 1984).

avoid the prospect of such conditions being overturned on appeal, planning authorities are increasingly having recourse to agreements for the purpose. Such agreements are commonly used to restrict the occupation of new houses in the countryside to agricultural workers. They are also being widely used to restrict the occupation of sheltered homes and retirement flats to people above a certain age. We have come across similar restrictions employed in connection with the occupation of commercial premises, a timber business, a "high tech" park, a market garden, a caretaker's house and "granny" flats. We have also been told of agreements restricting the use of a marina to members only and the use of car parks to the tenants of specified premises.

2. Agreements regulating the development of land

This category concerns development which is to be carried out in a certain way or subject to certain standards. This is by far the largest of the groupings.

In view of the number of agreements falling into this category, it seems to us that it might be helpful to attempt a further subdivision according to whether or not the obligation in question could be made the subject of a condition. In most cases, we are unable to say whether a particular obligation did, in fact, duplicate a condition because we did not see the related planning permission.

We think it wise to make two caveats about this subdivision. First of all, the validity of a condition will depend very much on the particular circumstances of the case. In many instances we could only guess at these. Secondly, there is considerable uncertainty about what matters may properly be made the subject of a condition. Because so much depends on the circumstances, guidance from the courts has tended to be given only in the most general terms. We were informed that the object of a number of agreements was to provide certainty in this twilight zone. Both these factors mean that here too the allocation of agreements to each subdivision is to some extent arbitrary.

(1) Duplicating conditions. Complete duplication of conditions was achieved by a clause we found in a number of agreements requiring the development to be carried out in accordance with the terms of the permission. Sometimes it was framed specifically in terms of an obligation to comply with the conditions on the planning permission. The advantage of such a clause is that it opens the door to alternative means of enforcing the conditions and the response to the questionnaires indicates that this is the second most important reason why planning agreements are used.[12]

Of the clauses which might have been duplicating individual conditions, one which appeared in several agreements was a provision imposing a time limit both for the commencement and completion of the development. The former is a standard condition on a planning permission.[13] The latter is rarely the subject of a condition partly because of practical difficulties associated with enforcement.[14] Service of a completion notice under section 41 of the 1972 Act may sometimes provide a way round the difficulty. Section 41 provides that planning permission for the development will cease to have effect after a stipulated time if the development has not been completed. There is, however, an opportunity for appealing against such a notice to the Secretary of State and a planning authority, concerned to ensure that the whole of a development is carried out, may prefer to deal with the matter in an agreement. The sanction for such a provision is generally a clause in the agreement providing for revocation of the permission without compensation in the event of default.

Time limits of a rather different sort were in some cases imposed by agreement on the carrying on of operations and uses. For example, in one case flight times from an airfield which was being developed were curtailed for the benefit of neighbours. In another case, the conduct of blasting operations in extending a quarry was similarly curtailed.

Other limits which were imposed by agreement with a view to regulating the way in which development was carried on included limits on the amount of material which might be extracted from a quarry over a prescribed period, on the number of caravans on a caravan site, on the period of occupancy of caravans and chalets in any one year,[15] on the bed spaces in a time share scheme, on the houses to be built on a site, on the amount of retail floor space in a retail unit, on the scale of operations in a light industrial development, on the number of motor coaches which might operate from a garage, on the numbers of cars which might operate

---

[12] SDD Circular 18/1986 advises that where a problem posed by a development proposal may be solved equally well either by condition or agreement, authorities should deal with the problem by way of condition because the use of an agreement deprives the developer of the opportunity to have the restriction varied or removed by way of appeal to the Secretary of State (para. 10).

[13] See ss. 38 and 39 of the 1972 Act.

[14] See also SDD Circular 18/1986, para. 18; and, *F. Lucas & Sons Ltd.* v. *Dorking and Horley RDC* (1964) 17 P. & C.R. 111.

[15] See SDD Circular 18/1986, para. 91.

from a driving school, on the size of service vehicles which might deliver to shops, on the method of heating food in a restaurant, on the sale of alcohol at a distillery and on the percentage of retail sales from wholesale premises. In a number of cases, limits were imposed on permissible levels of pollution, particularly noise but also chemical emissions. One advantage of dealing with the last of these by way of agreement is the opportunity provided for setting out detailed and complex monitoring requirements, the sort of provision which does not fit easily into a grant of planning permission.

Another form of limitation which we came across in an agreement dealt with the composition of the workforce for a development. The development in question was the construction of a petrochemical complex and the agreement required the developers to give a "full and fair opportunity", all other factors being equal, to local subcontractors and local labour to supply goods and provide the services necessary for the construction of the plant. The agreement went on to require the developers to give preference in the selection of their permanent workforce to local contractors and residents, again, all other factors being equal. A condition on a planning permission in these terms would be likely to be regarded as unreasonable unless it was supported by a particularly strong planning policy.

Provided that the overall purpose of the agreement remains regulatory, the Secretary of State has expressed the view that obligations of a positive nature may be imposed.[16] In practice such obligations have been widely imposed. Typically, they deal with such matters as the protection of trees during building or engineering operations, the provision of fencing around a site, the laying out of an access or car park and the carrying out of landscaping. Such obligations are often coupled with a continuing maintenance requirement, particularly where open space associated with a large housing scheme is not being taken over by a local authority. Other examples of a maintenance obligation include a case where a new dwelling was allowed to be built in the grounds of an existing dwelling and the developer agreed to maintain the access in good condition and subject to good visibility for all time coming; and a case where roads not constructed to an adequate standard for adoption were to be maintained. In the past, there has been some uncertainty about whether a condition may properly impose a continuing maintenance obligation on a developer. Ministry of Housing and Local Government Circular no. 5/68, for example,

---

[16] See SDD Circular 22/1984, para. 9 and Chap. 3.

expressed some doubts about this.[17] SDD Circular 18/1986 still expresses reservations about the imposition of maintenance conditions on a grant of planning permission for the erection of buildings or other works other than works of a continuing nature such as minerals extraction.[18] We find it difficult to see what objection there could be to a condition which imposes a maintenance obligation for so long as a development lasts in cases where maintenance—for example of fencing—is considered an important factor in the assimilation of a development into the landscape.

A continuing maintenance obligation of the kind just described is one of a number of provisions we have come across which are concerned not so much with the initial execution of the development but with its management thereafter. Other examples we have seen include the operation of traffic management schemes in connection with retail developments, the use of a specified access or egress, management schemes for a science park, for a car park, for a multi-purpose open air recreational centre, for a chalet development, for a sheltered housing scheme, and for an established tree belt screening a development, the monitoring of pollution levels, operational safeguards at a pipe treatment works, and in one case, an undertaking to keep members of the public away from the top of a quarry.

A condition requiring the restoration of a site on completion of development seems to be perfectly acceptable and is to be found as a matter of course in most mineral permissions; and the Town and Country Planning (Minerals) Act 1981 now allows for the imposition of after care conditions.[19] The advantage of an alternative means of enforcement, particularly the prospect of being able readily to take direct action in default, has made restoration an attractive subject for section 50 agreements and all those dealing with mineral operations that we have seen have included such an obligation.

There is a further advantage in dealing with restoration by way of agreement and that is the level of detail and degree of flexibility which can be achieved. This is well illustrated in a series of agreements which dealt with the construction of the landfall section of pipelines from the North Sea together with associated works. One in particular made extensive provision for the restoration of dunes and the bed of a loch whilst allowing for much of the detail to be settled to the satisfaction of the planning authority at the time the work was undertaken.

---

[17] "The Use of Conditions on Planning Permissions," para. 33.
[18] Para. 68.
[19] s. 22.

The ability of a section 50 agreement to impose detailed obligations whilst retaining a degree of flexibility has emerged as one of the most important advantages of this approach to the control of development. It has been applied not only to restoration on completion of development but in other areas as well. For example, much of the detail of major schemes of development can only be settled once the scheme is under way. The provisions in the 1972 Act and in the General Development Order for reserved matters applications cater for some but not all of these.[20] Planning authorities generally attempt to deal with matters of detail which fall outside the definition of reserved matters[21] by way of conditional conditions but the degree of specificity required can make this an unsatisfactory mechanism. A number of planning authorities have got round this problem and have gained the advantage of flexibility by using section 50 agreements to control outstanding areas of detail. We have seen such provisions, for example, in agreements dealing with the building of retail warehouses, the establishment of shopping developments, the carrying out of large housing schemes, the digging of a mine shaft, the building of a petrochemical complex, the erection of a hotel and leisure complex, and the construction of the landfall section of pipelines from the North Sea.

A rather different area where the need for flexibility has been demonstrated is in the phasing of development. Phasing is a matter which it is difficult to cover adequately in a condition.[22] Flexibility is required, enforcement is difficult and the phasing may be linked to matters which are not related to the subject matter of the application, are beyond the control of the applicant, and arguably would be beyond the proper scope of a condition. Provisions of this nature (which we have seen in a large number of agreements) straddle the boundary between obligations which duplicate conditions and those which go beyond conditions. Most commonly, phasing is concerned with linking residential development to the provision of supporting services such as roads and drainage. Sometimes agreements are used to ensure that landscaping, open space and other community facilities are available before completion of all or a prescribed part of a residential scheme. And we have seen agreements linking the phasing of retail developments to the provision of industrial floor space. In several cases, the

---

[20] See ss. 39 and 40 of the 1972 Act and arts. 8, 9 and 16 of the Town and Country Planning (General Development) (Scotland) Order 1981.

[21] Art. 2 of the General Development Order; and see *Inverclyde District Council* v. *Inverkip Building Co.*, 1983 S.L.T. 563.

[22] But see SDD Circular 18/1986, paras. 57–58.

demolition of existing buildings was tied in to the development of the site.[23] In a number of cases relating to mineral workings new excavation was tied to the restoration of worked out areas. The development of a fish farm was tied to the provision of shore based facilities. In another case landscaping was to be completed before a car sales area was established. In a further case the cinema part of a proposed entertainment complex was to be brought into use before or at the same time as the remainder. In two cases, agreements were used to co-ordinate the development of an area by several different developers. Agreements dealing with the construction of the landfall section of pipelines from the North Sea required a number of matters to be settled before work could commence—for example, the preparation of an environmental impact statement and of an emergency plan to cope with hazardous incidents. The latter provision also appeared in an agreement dealing with the construction of a petrochemical complex.

A further obligation which straddles the boundary between proper and improper conditions is that requiring the provision on site of some facility not included in the planning application but nonetheless linked to the development for which application is being made. The planning authority may be minded, for example, to grant planning permission for residential or retail development subject to the provision of a children's play area. It is difficult to determine at what stage the authority ceases to "regulate" the development to be carried out.[24] The difficulty in such cases can be overcome by requesting the developer to submit an amended application. However, this may be regarded as unduly cumbersome and an alternative approach which appears to have been adopted in connection with a number of schemes is to conclude an agreement under section 50 covering such matters.

(2) Beyond conditions. The response to our questionnaires showed that, overwhelmingly, the reason for most planning agreements was to enable planning authorities to extend their development control powers to regulate matters which are beyond the proper

---

[23] The Local Government and Planning (Scotland) Act 1982 makes specific provision for the imposition of conditions linking the demolition of listed buildings to the redevelopment of the site (Sched. 2, para. 15).

[24] Contrast *M.J. Shanley Ltd. (in liquidation)* v. *Secretary of State for the Environment* [1982] J.P.L. 380, with *Brittania (Cheltenham) Ltd.* v. *Secretary of State for the Environment* [1978] J.P.L. 554; see also *Hall & Co. Ltd.* v. *Shoreham-by-Sea UDC* [1964] 1 W.L.R. 240; *Westminster Renslade Ltd.* v. *Secretary of State for the Environment* [1983] J.P.L. 455; and *Bradford City Metropolitan Council* v. *Secretary of State for the Environment* [1986] J.P.L. 598.

scope of conditions. Examples of these sorts of obligation are described in this section.

While planning control may overlap with other public controls over land,[25] a condition on a planning permission specifically requiring compliance with other controls is likely to be regarded as unnecessary and unenforceable.[26] In several cases this sort of obligation has been imposed by agreement. For example, an agreement dealing with the development of an airfield included an undertaking by the developers to comply with all statutory and other regulations relating to the development and use of the airfield and obliged the developers to use their best endeavours to ensure that their agents and all users of the airfield complied with such controls. In another case, the conversion of existing buildings into four separate residential units was made subject to compliance with building warrant. And in other cases, estate roads and on-site drainage and water supply were to be constructed in accordance with the requirements of the appropriate service departments of the district and regional councils.

It is questionable just how far agreements may go in this direction. They must, after all, be "planning" agreements.[27] While there is inevitably an overlap between planning and other controls, it is difficult to see that a requirement, for example, to comply with regulations made under the Health and Safety at Work etc. Act 1974 or to pay fair wages (both of which we have seen) could be said to be serving a planning purpose.

Though it seems that conditions may properly control not only the use but also the occupancy of land, it is very doubtful whether they can trespass into matters of title. As we mentioned earlier in this chapter, this might well be regarded by the courts as an undue interference in property rights. Yet there may be good planning reasons for seeking to do this. Development may only be acceptable if the planning authority has some guarantee that a particular state of affairs will continue. A number of authorities have used section 50 agreements to overcome this difficulty. For example, on several occasions where new dwellings were allowed in the grounds of

---

[25] See, e.g. Esdell Caravan Parks Ltd. v. Hemel Hempstead RDC [1966] 1 Q.B. 895; Hanks v. Minister of Housing and Local Government [1963] 1 Q.B. 999; Westminster Bank Ltd. v. Minister of Housing and Local Government [1971] A.C. 508; and Ladbroke (Rentals) Ltd. v. Secretary of State for the Environment [1981] J.P.L. 427.

[26] See British Airports Authority and Others v. Secretary of State for Scotland and Another 1979 S.C. 200; 1979 S.L.T. 197. Also SDD Circular 18/1986, paras. 22–24.

[27] See R. v. Gillingham Borough Council, ex p. F. Parham Ltd. [1988] J.P.L. 336.

existing dwellings, the owners agreed to incorporate into any conveyance of the land for the new dwellings a heritable and irredeemable servitude right of access over a prescribed area. One of these agreements also required the conveyance of a one half *pro indiviso* share of an existing double garage.

The upkeep of common amenity areas on residential estates provides a further example of title requirements in agreements being used to overcome planning problems. In a number of cases, developers agreed to execute a deed of conditions or to insert a condition in missives of sale and in the subsequent dispositions imposing an obligation on future owners to pay a proportion of the cost of the upkeep of such areas. In another case, the agreement merely imposed an obligation on the developer to make arrangements for the satisfactory handing on of responsibility for the maintenance of these amenity areas on completion of the development.

A title provision of a rather different sort is that requiring a developer to acquire land or a right over land outside his control for the purpose of his development. A positive condition to this effect on the planning permission would be *ultra vires* as being possibly incapable of fulfilment and of enforcement.[28] The use of an agreement in this case will avoid a refusal of permission. In one case, where planning permission was granted for an extension of a quarry, the developer agreed to acquire land to improve the access and to use his best endeavours to acquire land for landscaping. A similar provision regarding the acquisition of land for landscaping appeared in an agreement dealing with the construction of a petrochemical complex. A further agreement, also dealing with an extension to a quarry, required a developer to secure from a third party a right of access for vehicles. In another case, planning permission for the development of a mine shaft and ancillary buildings was subject to satisfactory arrangements being concluded with a third party for the disposal of spoil on that party's land. The same agreement also required the developer to secure the vacation, temporarily or permanently, of residential properties in the vicinity of the works which would be affected by an intolerable level of noise and to buy up some of those properties. A proposed agreement linked to applications for gas fractination and ethylene plants required the developer to secure the agreement of all parties

---

[28] *British Airports Authority* v. *Secretary of State for Scotland, cit. supra; Birnie* v. *Banff County Council*, 1954 S.L.T (Sh.Ct.) 90. But see *Grampian Regional Council* v. *City of Aberdeen District Council*, 1984 S.L.T. 197. Also SDD Circular 18/1986 paras. 29 and 37.

having an interest in land included in a safety zone around the site to the regulation of the use of such land. In a number of cases, the sight lines required for the junction of an access to development with the nearest public road depended on the owners of the neighbouring land accepting restrictions on the use of the land affected by the sight lines and this was provided for by agreement.

We have also come across agreements requiring, not the acquisition of land, but the cession of land by developers generally to local authorities for the provision of services to support the development.[29] Agreements have been employed, for example, to secure the provision of land for the construction of schools, community facilities and sewage pumping stations, for public road improvements and for the laying out of public open space and car parking. Such agreements sometimes also require the cession of the land to the local authority at a price considerably less than its full market value.[30]

Quite a number of agreements we have seen imposed obligations on developers to carry out works on land outwith their control, obligations clearly beyond the scope of conditions. For example, several agreements required developers to arrange for improvements to the public road system or to undertake landscaping made necessary by their development. Another required the developer to construct a footpath on land belonging to the planning authority on the perimeter of the site being developed. A second required a scheme for recreational development linked to a housing scheme to be carried out by the developer on land belonging to the planning authority. A third required the provision of a labour camp, in a location to be approved by the planning authority, to house the temporary workforce engaged upon the development.

In similar vein, another agreement required a developer to provide and operate a free bus service linking the supermarket for which permission was being granted to residential estates.

An alternative approach to off-site works which is commonly adopted is to require the developer to pay the cost of someone else (usually a local authority) carrying out such works, again an

---

[29] It is a well-established principle that no payment of money or other consideration can be required when granting planning permission. SDD Circular 18/1986 states that conditions to this effect should not be attached to planning permissions (para. 69).

[30] The price to be paid by a local authority possessing compulsory purchase powers would normally be determined under the provisions of the Land Compensation (Scotland) Act 1963. This provides for compensation based on the market value of the land. See on this J. Rowan-Robinson and M. G. Lloyd, *Land Development and the Infrastructure Lottery* (T. & T. Clark Ltd., 1988), Chaps. 3 and 4.

obligation which appears to be beyond the scope of a condition.[31] SDD Circular 22/1984 says of such obligations that "while the developer may reasonably be expected to pay for or contribute to the cost of infrastructure which would not have been necessary but for his development, and while some public benefit may eventually accrue from this, his payments should be directly related in scale and kind to the benefit which the proposed development will derive from the facilities to be provided."[32] Such obligations have required developers to pay for the provision by the local authority of public car parking spaces, to reimburse the cost of drainage facilities, to pay in full or to contribute towards the cost of public road and bridge improvements, to meet the cost of future maintenance of public open space and, in one case, to reimburse the cost of the provision of hedging by the regional council on the verge of a main road running along the boundary of a site. Several developers involved in the major expansion of a village were required to enter into similar agreements providing for the payment of contributions to the planning authority to meet the cost of laying out a central open space.

A more indirect sort of financial obligation imposed in many cases was a requirement to provide security for the fulfilment of conditions on the grant of planning permission. Typically such agreements were linked to permissions for mineral working and ensured the carrying out of restoration works in due course. Planning permission for the construction of the landfall section of a North Sea gas pipeline through sand dunes and a loch was accompanied by an agreement setting out extensive requirements as regards landscaping and restoration, the whole to be supported by a fiduciary guarantee.

A financial guarantee of a different sort was provided by agreements which required the several developers involved in a scheme for the major expansion of a village to contribute towards a fund to be maintained by the planning authority. The purpose of the fund was to provide some guarantee for the regional council that the scheme would be implemented so as to make full use of sewerage and water supply facilities being provided by them and the scheme would be phased to tie in with the authority's programme for the provision of these facilities.

---

[31] *R. v. Bowman* [1898] 1 Q.B. 663. And see the discussion in M. Grant, *Urban Planning Law* (Sweet and Maxwell, 1982, 1st supplement, 1986), pp. 343–345; also SDD Circular 18/1986, para. 69. See also J. Rowan-Robinson and M. G. Lloyd, *Land Development and the Infrastructure Lottery, supra*, Chaps. 3 and 4.

[32] Para. 15.

3. Agreements restricting the use of land

Within this category are those agreements which impose some prohibition or limitation on the existing use of land.

The Town and Country Planning (Scotland) Act 1947 took away the landowner's inherent right to develop land. Subsequent legislation set up a complex scheme of compensation for the loss of this right.[33] Since then a licence, in the form of a grant of planning permission, has been required before development can take place. A refusal or conditional grant of permission does not infringe any of the legal rights of a landowner and does not, therefore, normally give rise to a right to compensation. The 1947 Act left the landowner with the right to continue the existing use of land. Any attempt by the planning authority to control the *existing* use of the land is an infringement of proprietary rights and the general scheme of the legislation is that when such control is exercised[34] it is subject to the payment of compensation.[35]

There will be occasions when a planning authority is unwilling to permit new development unless an existing use of land is restricted. Such restrictions would normally give rise to a liability to pay compensation and the planning authority might be unwilling to countenance the new development on such a basis. It would seem that, in some instances, this sort of restriction may be imposed by way of condition on the grant of permission for the new development, thus avoiding payment of compensation.[36] However, to avoid uncertainty, some authorities prefer to proceed by means of a section 50 agreement which enables the parties to agree to the imposition of restrictions on the existing use without compensation in return for a grant of planning permission for the new development.

---

[33] See now Pt. VII of the Town and Country Planning (Scotland) Act 1972. In a consultation paper issued in April 1986, the SDD proposed the repeal of Pt. VII of the Act.

[34] *e.g.* by means of revocation order (s. 42 of the 1972 Act), a discontinuance order (s. 49 of the 1972 Act), a direction under art. 4 of the Town and Country Planning (General Development) (Scotland) Order 1981, or a refusal or conditional grant of planning permission for any of the categories of development in Pt. II of Sched. 6 to the 1972 Act.

[35] See, *e.g.* ss. 153, 154, 158 and 159 of the 1972 Act. The compensation provisions are currently under review (see the consultation paper issued by SDD in April 1986).

[36] *Kingston-upon-Thames Royal London Borough Council* v. *Secretary of State for the Environment* [1973] 1 W.L.R. 169; *British Airports Authority* v. *Secretary of State for Scotland per* the Lord President (Lord Emslie), 1979 S.C. 200; 1979 S.L.T. 197; *cf. Hartnell* v. *Minister of Housing and Local Government* [1965] A.C. 1134; and *Allnatt London Properties* v. *Middlesex County Council* (1964) 15 P. & C.R. 288.

The most frequent use of agreements for this purpose has been to revoke an existing, but as yet unimplemented, permission for the development of land in return for a new permission for development of the land. This avoids any question as to whether both permissions can be implemented in whole or part. There is, in fact, a procedure set out in section 43 of the 1972 Act for unopposed revocation of an existing permission which excludes the payment of compensation. However, the procedure under section 43 is cumbersome and many authorities seem to prefer the device of a simple agreement.[37]

Agreements have also been used quite commonly to secure the discontinuance of the existing use of premises on the grant of permission for a similar use at new premises.[38] On several occasions, for example, permission has been granted by authorities for a new dwelling in return for the discontinuance of the use of an existing, generally substandard, dwelling and, sometimes, its subsequent demolition. We have also come across agreements restricting the existing use of land and/or buildings as workshops, a quarry, offices, a hot food carry out, scrap metal businesses, a wholesale and retail builders merchant, and amusement arcades in return for replacement permissions relating to other land or buildings. Other cases include agreements providing for the discontinuance of permission for a retail complex upon its relocation on another site, for the discontinuance of the use of a high level vehicle track in a National Scenic Area in return for planning permission for an alternative line for the track, for the replacement of three radio masts by one, and for the construction of a new dwelling house in return for the discontinuance of a commercial haulage business coupled with the demolition of a barn and the restoration of the site.

A number of agreements we have seen are related to the grant of planning permission for a new dwelling for an agricultural worker on a farm. The agreements impose restrictions on the categories of people who may occupy the *existing* dwellings on the farm. Harsh as such a restriction may seem, it is tied in with the general policy which prevailed in many rural areas of limiting new dwellings to those required to meet a local need. The restriction is intended to discourage any attempt to get round strict policies of this kind by moving agricultural workers from an existing

---

[37] In *West Oxfordshire District Council* v. *Secretary of State for the Environment* [1988] J.P.L. 324, Graham Eyre, Q.C., sitting as deputy judge, observed that the right conveyed by a grant of planning permission could be surrendered or modified by a planning agreement.

[38] *Ibid.*

dwelling into a new dwelling and then disposing of the existing dwelling on the open market.

4. *Agreements regulating the use of land*

This category is concerned with agreements which provide for an existing use to be carried on in a certain way or subject to certain standards. We have only come across a few agreements of this type.

On two occasions agreements were entered into providing for the relaxation of the standard condition relating to occupation of a dwelling by an agricultural worker. The agreements provided that in the event of it being demonstrated that there was no longer a demand or need for the dwelling from people employed in agriculture, the dwelling might be sold to persons who could not satisfy the agricultural occupancy condition. Such agreements are now unnecessary following the bringing into force of the provision in Schedule 2 to the Local Government and Planning (Scotland) Act 1982 which permits the making of an application for permission to continue development free from specified conditions. In somewhat similar fashion another agreement provided for the temporary relaxation of a condition limiting the classes of goods which could be sold from two retail warehouses.

On occasions, the opportunity has been taken of a planning application to extend quarrying operations to secure an agreement tidying up control of present and future workings on the existing site. And in two instances, agreements have been employed to regulate the swapping of uses between premises (from shops to offices and vice versa).

On several occasions planning authorities took advantage of the opportunity provided by an application for planning permission to secure, through the medium of a section 50 agreement, some regulation of the use of the applicant's land for the benefit of the public. In a number of cases, applicants undertook to upgrade listed buildings within their control located on or near the application sites. In one case, residential development of part of a woodland was made subject to the preparation of a management plan for the remainder of the woodland and to the provision of public access. In another, permission to subdivide a large house on the shores of Loch Lomond into a number of flats was linked to an agreement allowing the planning authority to construct and maintain a public walkway through the site. In the third case, planning permission for the construction of a dwelling house, again on the shores of Loch Lomond, was linked to an agreement providing, amongst other things, for public access over a defined area. And in two other cases, provision was made for a riverside walkway and for a footpath for use by the public in consideration of planning permission for development.

Development control or planning gain?

All the section 50 agreements that we have come across have been linked in one way or another to the operation of the development control system. The great majority of these have arisen in response to an application for planning permission but the motives behind the agreements have varied.

Some agreements were used merely to give emphasis to the conditions on the planning permissions; others appear to have been used to avoid the prospect of a successful appeal to the Secretary of State against a condition or to secure an alternative means of enforcement either through the courts or by direct action. Many resulted from uncertainty about the validity of particular conditions and many more sought to control matters which were clearly beyond the scope of conditions. Quite a few, clearly motivated by the scale of complexity of the development proposed, sought a degree of flexibility of control and management of the development beyond the normal range of a planning permission. Several were used to overcome objections to the development which would otherwise have led to its refusal, for example, the need to restrict or regulate land outwith the applicant's control or to tie the development in with provision of public services. A few were apparently prompted by doubts about the financial stability of the developer or by his poor record of compliance with conditions on earlier planning permissions.

Not all agreements that we are aware of have arisen in response to planning applications. In several cases planning authorities have used them as the vehicle for accomplishing the relocation of non-conforming uses, the expenses of relocation being borne by the authority. And in three instances agreements were used for enforcement purposes. In one case an enforcement notice and a stop notice relating to unauthorised tipping were withdrawn in return for an undertaking to discontinue tipping and to carry out landscaping. In another, a house which had been built in the wrong place was granted retrospective planning permission in return for the revocation of the original permission and an agreement not to develop the site further. In the third case an enforcement notice had been served in respect of an unauthorised extension to a dwelling. An appeal against the notice had been lodged with the Secretary of State. The matter was resolved by way of an agreement in which the owner undertook to carry out certain alterations to the extension within a stipulated time.

Although all the agreements that we are aware of have been linked in some way to the operation of the development control system, a few of these have been less concerned with the control of a particular development than with securing what might be described as a "planning gain." The concept of "planning gain" is discussed in some detail in Chapter 10. It has been variously defined. The Property Advisory Group, who were very critical of the pursuit of planning gain, defined it as a benefit which could not validly be obtained by way of a condition on a planning permission.[39] Obviously, in this sense, a great many of the obligations imposed by section 50 agreements which have been discussed in this chapter constitute a planning gain.

We consider this definition to be too broad to be useful. Indeed, the Property Advisory Group, having criticised the pursuit of planning gain (in the sense in which they used that phrase), were then forced to make some sweeping exceptions. What most people seem to have in mind when they talk of planning gain is some sort of benefit to the community which was not part of the original proposal by a developer, and was therefore negotiated, and is not of itself of any commercial advantage to the developer.

Even this definition embraces many obligations imposed essentially for the purpose of development control. In particular, it would include quite a large number of agreements the principal object of which has been to secure the adequate provision of supporting services (for example, public roads, main drains, car parking, open space, and community facilities) for the developments proposed. We are seeking to make a distinction here between such obligations and those which seek some other advantage largely unconnected with the control of the development itself. For the purposes of this chapter we therefore define planning gain as an obligation undertaken by a developer which does not form a part of or contribute to the development. It is clearly something which could not be the subject of a condition as it would not be, in the strict sense of the term, "related to the subject matter of the application";[40] and it would appear to be something which conflicts with the policy advice on the scope of planning agreements contained in SDD Circular 22/1984 (paras. 11–16).

---

[39] Property Advisory Group, *Planning Gain* (HMSO, 1981), para. 3.01.
[40] See *Pyx Granite Co.* v. *Minister of Housing and Local Government* [1960] A.C. 260; *Newbury District Council* v. *Secretary of State for the Environment* [1980] 1 All E.R. 731; *British Airports Authority* v. *Secretary of State for Scotland*, 1979 S.C. 200; 1979 S.L.T. 197.

One of the interesting points to emerge from the 1987 survey is the increasing use of agreements by planning authorities to secure planning gain. It would be an overstatement to describe this as a trend but there have been some notable examples, particularly those linked to proposals for major retail developments. For example, during the public inquiry into the proposed regional shopping and leisure centre at the former Leyland Vehicle Plant at Bathgate counsel for the applicants announced that, in addition to meeting the cost of supporting services, a substantial area of industrial floor space (approx. 20,900 sq.m.) would be made available with ancillary facilities to replace that to be taken up for the shopping and leisure centre. And we are aware of a number of concluded agreements linked to major retailing proposals which make provision for industrial floor space (with the commencement and continuation of retailing being tied in some instances to the commencement and continuation of the industrial use). Other agreements have linked retail developments variously to the provision of sport and leisure facilities, a hotel, a concert hall and a civic square.

Other examples of planning gain include permission for the development of an industrial site linked to the gifting of land to the district council for a golf course, and permission for residential development linked to the gifting of a nature conservation site to the local authority. In several cases planning authorities have taken the opportunity presented by a proposal to develop land to obtain controlled public access to a scenic area. In one of these cases, which involved the development of part of a woodland, the agreement also secured the preparation of a management plan for the remainder of the woodland. In several other cases advantage was taken of proposals to build, improve or extend property to ensure the carrying out of works of maintenance or repair to buildings of historic or architectural interest. An agreement for a petrochemical complex imposed an obligation on the developer to discriminate in favour of local people in the selection of the workforce required for the construction and operation of the plant. The same agreement provided that if the development did not proceed the developer was to offer the land for sale to the local authority. In several other cases an application for new development was seen as presenting an opportunity to secure the discontinuance of an existing non-conforming use on another site.

CHAPTER 9

OTHER POWERS

PLANNING by agreement, as we indicated in the Introduction, is
not conducted solely through the mechanism of section 50 of the
1972 Act. There are a considerable number of other statutory
powers which provide for the making of agreements governing the
use, development or management of land.

For the purposes of explanation, a broad and admittedly
somewhat arbitrary distinction can be drawn between agreements
which affect the carrying on of the existing use of the land and
those associated with proposals for the development of land. The
landowner's right to carry on the existing use of land was left
undisturbed by the advent of comprehensive planning control. If
a public authority wish to impose some restriction or obligation
upon this right, the general position is that the landowner, assuming
he or she is willing to accept the imposition at all, may expect to
be compensated for the restriction or to be paid to carry out the
obligation. Into this category of agreement fall those negotiated
by the Nature Conservancy Council in respect of national nature
reserves and sites of special scientific interest, those negotiated by
the Department of Agriculture and Fisheries for Scotland in
environmentally sensitive areas and agreements negotiated by
planning authorities for access to open country.

Since the advent of comprehensive planning control, landowners
have, however, had no right to develop their land. In order to do
so they must first obtain a licence from the state in the form of a
grant of planning permission. In order to obtain planning permission, the landowner may need to satisfy the planning authority on
certain matters such as landscaping, access and car parking, and
these, as we have already indicated, may in some circumstances
be tied up in an agreement under section 50 of the 1972 Act.
There will, however, be occasions where a section 50 agreement
cannot be used—for example, where the developer is not yet the
owner of the necessary land and the present landowner declines
to be a party to a section 50 agreement. In that event, some
planning authorities insist on an interim agreement with the
developer entered into under the general power contained in
section 69 of the Local Government (Scotland) Act 1973. Further-

more, in circumstances where there is no obligation on the public sector to provide essential supporting services for such development—for example, improvements to the public road network—the developer may have to make the necessary provision and the arrangements may be tied up in a statutory agreement. The essential characteristic of such agreements is that, far from receiving payment or compensation, the burden is borne by the developer. The agreements are a mechanism for removing obstacles to development. Falling into this category are agreements for public road improvements under section 48 of the Roads (Scotland) Act 1984 and for contributions towards main sewerage provision under section 8 of the Sewerage (Scotland) Act 1968.

There are, inevitably, a number of agreements which do not fall into either of the categories we have described above. These miscellaneous agreements include voluntary restrictions on land use agreed with the National Trust for Scotland, dedication agreements with the Forestry Commission and agreements with the Capital Taxes Office in connection with exemptions from inheritance tax.

The object of this chapter is to describe these other agreements which may affect the use, development or management of land.[1] These are grouped under the following headings:

Development Agreements
1. Local Government (Scotland) Act 1973, s. 69
2. Local Government (Scotland) Act 1973, s. 85
3. Infrastructure agreements
4. Private legislation

Existing Use Agreements
5. Nature Conservancy Council agreements
6. Scenic and recreational agreements
7. Environmentally sensitive area agreements

Miscellaneous Agreements
8. Conservation agreements with the National Trust for Scotland
9. Forestry dedication agreements
10. The countryside and capital taxation relief.

These agreements are now described in turn.

---

[1] This chapter is more in the nature of a chronicle than an analysis of these agreements. It does not purport to list all the statutory powers, merely the more obvious ones.

Development Agreements

1. *Local Government (Scotland) Act 1973, s. 69*

As is mentioned earlier in this book, if a planning authority for the better discharge of their functions wish to enter into an agreement with any other party, there is nothing to prevent them from so doing.[2] Any such agreement would be enforceable in the normal way by the parties to it. Local authorities have always had power to do anything which can reasonably be regarded as incidental to the discharge of their functions.[3] That power was given statutory recognition in section 69 of the Local Government (Scotland) Act 1973, which empowers a local authority "to do anything (whether or not involving expenditure, borrowing or lending of money, or the acquisition or disposal of any property or rights) which is calculated to facilitate or is conducive or incidental to[4] the discharge of any of their functions." This would be sufficient authority for entering into an agreement for planning purposes. As SDD Circular 22/1984 observes, the section would "enable agreements to be made, which would not have to be limited in their purpose to restricting or regulating the development or use of land, for the payment of money or the transfer of assets to a local authority where this would facilitate the discharge of the functions of the authority." Section 69, does not, however, empower authorities to enter into agreements directed at industrial promotion.[5] Recourse should be had to section 154A of the 1973 Act instead.

Jones v. *Secretary of State for Wales*[6] appears to support the view that financial arrangements between a prospective developer who does not have any interest in the land in question and a local authority can be valid in terms of this statutory power. It may therefore be possible under section 69 to achieve certain of the purposes for which section 50 agreements are employed. An agreement under section 69 will not, of course, bind the land but that might not be a matter of concern to the planning authority in

---

[2] See Chap. 1.

[3] See *Attorney-General* v. *Great Eastern Railway Co.* (1880) 5 App. Cas. 473; *Graham* v. *Glasgow Corporation*, 1936 S.C. 108; and *Lawrence Building Co.* v. *Lanarkshire County Council*, 1979 S.L.T. 2.

[4] In *Meek* v. *Lothian Regional Council*, 1980 S.L.T. (Notes) 61, Lord McDonald in the Outer House accepted that "incidental to" should be given a narrow meaning and was not equivalent to "in connection with."

[5] Section 69(4) added by the Local Government and Planning (Scotland) Act 1982, Sched. 3 para. 16. For the meaning of "industrial promotion" see s. 154A(1) of the 1973 Act.

[6] (1974) 72 L.G.R. 583.

a case where the agreement is not designed to be of a long term nature but provides for an immediate and once and for all benefit to be provided by the developer. It may be that a planning authority is entitled to receive direct benefits under section 69 of the 1973 Act. Use of section 69 of the 1973 Act, in conjunction perhaps with section 50 of the 1972 Act, might provide the answer to possible problems with provision of infrastructure by a developer (see Chapters 1 and 3 *supra*). For example, there would appear to be no reason why a linked agreement of this sort should not contain a financial provision requiring a developer to contribute towards the cost of providing the infrastructure associated with his development. The incentive for the developer to accept such an obligation would be the related grant of planning permission and both tiers of planning authority could be joined as parties where appropriate.

One regional council has on at least two occasions entered into formal agreements with landowners under section 69 of the 1973 Act. In both cases planning permission had been granted for the use of the land in question for large scale residential development. The agreements provide that the landowners *or their successors in title* are to make over to the authority, at a fixed price, land required for educational or roads purposes. One of the agreements was backed by a bond taken out by the developers. In terms of the bond the developer is to reimburse to the regional authority any sum which the region may have to pay over and above the fixed price mentioned in the agreement. We have doubts as to whether these agreements are any more than personal contracts,[7] but it may be that the bond means that the arrangement can successfully achieve its purpose.

2. *Local Government (Scotland) Act 1973, s. 85*

Section 85 of the Local Government (Scotland) Act 1973 enables a local authority to "accept, hold and administer . . . for the purposes of any of their functions, gifts of property, whether heritable or moveable, made for that purpose . . ." On the face of it, section 85 might seem to provide a way of overcoming some of the difficulties which we believe could arise in connection with the use of section 50 powers in connection with arrangements involving some benefit to the authority, such as the dedication of land or buildings to the authority or the reimbursement of the cost of works undertaken by the authority.[8]

---

[7] See *Campbell's Trs.* v. *Glasgow Corporation* (1902) 4 F. 752 (Chap. 1 *supra*).
[8] See Chap. 3.

However, the decision in *County and District Properties* v. *Horsham Urban District Council*[9] seems to show that section 85 is of no assistance in such circumstances. In that case developers had made a payment of £6,000 to the local authority in connection with the provision of car parking by the authority on the understanding that planning permission would be granted for a certain development. A question arose as to the local authority's obligation to provide car parking. The document under which the £6,000 was paid was headed a deed of gift and the authority argued that the money should be treated as a gift under section 268 of the Local Government Act 1933 (which was very similar in its terms to section 85 of the Local Government (Scotland) Act 1973). Paull J. said that to apply such a description to this payment was a complete misuse of the word "gift" and a misunderstanding of the council's powers. He stated that the statute "contemplated a charitable gift by a charitably-minded person to benefit a district." It did not mean money paid as an inducement for the favourable consideration of a project which, if granted, would put large sums of money into the donor's pockets. However, distinguishing between a charitable gift and an inducement may not always be as easy as it appears to have been in this case.

3. Infrastructure agreements

Provision is made in a number of Acts for agreements dealing with infrastructure requirements arising from land development proposals.[10] The essential characteristic of these agreements is that the initiative comes from the developer. It is the developer who is seeking to secure the provision of essential supporting services for his development. This means that any consideration which is the subject of such an agreement is likely to flow from the developer to the local authority that he is seeking to persuade to provide the service. The scope of such agreements would appear to overlap to a considerable extent with that of agreements concluded under section 50 of the Town and Country Planning (Scotland) Act 1972.

(1) Roads (Scotland) Act 1984, s. 48. A proposal for the development of land may require improvements to be made to the public road network to cope with the additional traffic that will be generated. An applicant for planning permission cannot be re-

---

[9] (1970) 215 E.G. 1399.

[10] See in connection with these agreements J. Rowan-Robinson and M. G. Lloyd, *Land Development and the Infrastructure Lottery* (T. & T. Clark Ltd., 1988), Chaps. 3 and 4.

quired to undertake such improvements as a condition of the permission. Neither, it would seem, are the roads authority under any obligation to effect the necessary improvements although they have power to do so. If the improvements are not contained in the authority's capital programme, they are unlikely to be persuaded to exercise the power unless the developer is prepared to contribute some or all of the cost. Yet in the absence of such improvements it may well be that planning permission will be refused. Because of this, the developer may be willing to assume the burden and such an arrangement may be tied up by way of an agreement between the roads authority and the developer under section 48 of the Roads (Scotland) Act 1984. This enables the roads authority to enter into an agreement "with any person willing to contribute to the construction or improvement of the road."

Whilst such an agreement may be suitable for an immediate one-off payment, the difficulty is that it cannot be enforced against anyone other than the contracting party. Having obtained planning permission on the strength of such an agreement, the applicant could dispose of the land to someone else to carry out the development and the obligations in the agreement would not bind such a person. As a result, we found little evidence of the use of section 48 agreements, most authorities preferring to use the power in section 50 of the Town and Country Planning (Scotland) Act 1972 to deal with such matters because of the ability to enforce obligations against singular successors.

(2) Sewerage (Scotland) Act 1968. Section 1 of the 1968 Act imposes a duty on sewerage authorities, the regional and islands councils, to provide such sewers as may be necessary for effectually draining their areas of domestic sewage, surface water and trade effluent and to provide such treatment works etc. as may be required. This duty does not, however, require the authorities to do anything that is not practicable at a reasonable cost. The authorities are the judges, in the first instance, of what is reasonable.

Where, as happens not infrequently, a main sewer required for a scheme of development cannot be provided at a reasonable cost, the developer will have to face up to either meeting the excess cost or abandoning the scheme. Where a developer agrees to meet the excess, such an arrangement may be tied up by way of an agreement under section 8 of the 1968 Act.

Although the duty in section 1 of the Act extends to the reception and treatment of trade effluent, the Act gives sewerage authorities control over new discharges of such effluent. Section 26 subjects discharges to a licensing process. Many authorities, however, prefer to use the more flexible alternative of an agreement under section 37 of the Act. Such an agreement, which is entered into between the local authority and the owner or occupier of trade premises, provides for the treatment and disposal by the authority of the effluent and may also provide for the construction of any treatment works to cope with the new discharge and the repayment in whole or part by the owner or occupier of the authority's expenses in making such provision.

(3) Water (Scotland) Act 1980. Section 6 of the 1980 Act imposes a duty on water authorities, the regional and islands councils, to provide a supply of wholesome water to every part of their areas where this is required for *domestic* purposes and can be provided at a reasonable cost. The authorities are the judges, in the first instance, of what is reasonable and it seems that, as a matter of practice, such provision can generally be made at a reasonable cost.

Although section 9 of the Act requires authorities to supply water on request for *non-domestic* purposes, the requirement is subject to two important provisos. First of all it only applies where the supply can be made without prejudicing existing commitments and anticipated future requirements for domestic purposes. Secondly, the supply may be subject to reasonable terms and conditions, including payment of the cost of bringing the supply to the site. The normal arrangement is for the water authority and the person requesting the supply to enter into what is known as a "revenue agreement" whereby the latter agrees to pay annually for 12 years a sum not exceeding one-eighth of the cost of providing and laying any necessary water main. There is deducted from each annual payment any revenue in the form of metered or rate income received in that year by the authority for that supply.

4. Private legislation

None of the Scottish authorities which responded to our questionnaires had made any use of Private Act powers. We suspect that very few, if any, Scottish planning authorities possess powers comparable to those taken by many English authorities in the 1960s (see Chapter 3 *supra*).

Existing Use Agreements

5. Nature Conservancy Council agreements

(1) Management agreements for National Nature Reserves. One of the most important functions of the Nature Conservancy Council (NCC) is to establish, maintain and manage national nature reserves throughout the United Kingdom.[11] Such reserves are "declared" under section 19 of the National Parks and Access to the Countryside Act 1949 or section 35 of the Wildlife and Countryside Act 1981. Nature reserves are defined in section 15 of the 1949 Act. They are places designated with two purposes in mind. They provide a means of preserving fauna and flora and the physical conditions in which they live and geographical and physiographical features of interest, and they provide an opportunity for studying and for undertaking research into such matters.

The principal means available to the NCC for safeguarding such sites are to purchase or lease them or to negotiate management agreements under section 16 of the 1949 Act with the landowners. Perhaps not surprisingly, in view of limited resources for land acquisition, most Scottish reserves are safeguarded through the medium of agreements.

The Annual Report of the NCC for the period from April 1, 1986 to March 31, 1987 gives some idea of just how much land in Scotland is subject to control through such agreements. Of the 67 national nature reserves in Scotland covering some 107,275 hectares of land, 51 of them, covering some 76,384 hectares are safeguarded in whole or in part by management agreements. By comparison there are 116 national nature reserves in England comprising 40,767 hectares, of which 39, covering some 13,475 hectares are safeguarded in whole or in part by management agreements. These figures indicate the very substantial size of some of the Scottish reserves. Amongst them are the Cairngorms reserve extending over some 25,949 hectares, Inverpolly in Highland Region covering some 10,857 hectares and Caelaverock in Dumfries and Galloway covering 5,501 hectares.

The NCC have a model form of agreement, the most important part of which is the "agreed management policy" which is adapted in each case to meet the particular circumstances. The policy will deal with such matters as restrictions on land reclamation, the grazing of animals, the planting and cutting of timber, the extraction of peat and minerals, and the extent to which hunting and shooting may be carried on. The agreement will also set out the arrangements for study and research, for wardening the land, and for the payment of a sum by way of compensation for these restrictions.

---

[11] Nature Conservancy Council Act 1973, s. 1.

The NCC have experienced few difficulties over the years in enforcing these agreements.

(2) Management agreements for Sites of Special Scientific Interest (SSSIs). There are many areas throughout the United Kingdom which are not managed as nature reserves but which, nonetheless, are, in the opinion of the NCC, of special interest by reason of their flora or fauna or because of their geological or physiographical features. Section 23 of the National Parks and Access to the Countryside Act 1949 imposed a duty on what is now the NCC to notify planning authorities of such sites so that these could be safeguarded from development.

By the end of 1981 about 4,136 such SSSIs had been notified in Great Britain, covering 1,377,956 hectares. However, evidence showed that the notification procedure was proving ineffective in safeguarding SSSIs from land use changes beyond planning control, notably agricultural and forestry operations.[12] Increasing public and parliamentary concern led to new provisions for SSSI protection being incorporated into Pt. II of the Wildlife and Countryside Act 1981. These provisions are based on a reciprocal notification procedure. The NCC must now notify owners and occupiers of land of the location of SSSIs, of the nature of the scientific interest and of any operations which are likely to damage that interest. Owners and occupiers must, in their turn, give advance notice to the NCC of a proposal to carry out any such potentially damaging operation. This imposes a temporary restraint on the operation and is intended to give the NCC an opportunity to reach agreement on ways of safeguarding the scientific interest.

Owners and occupiers are under no compulsion to fall in with the NCC's wishes. Nonetheless, the government believe that "the best guarantee of the future of Britain's landscape lies in the natural feel for it possessed by those who live and work in it. This is why the heart of the Wildlife and Countryside Act is fashioned from a policy of consent."[13] The key to this policy of consent is the management agreement concluded under section 15 of the Countryside Act 1968. Under such agreements owners and occupiers forgo the benefit of improvements to their land in return for compensation. The payment of compensation is a distinctive feature of the "voluntary" approach.

---

[12] P. Goode, "The Threat to Wildlife Habitats" (1981) 89 New Scientist 219.
[13] *The Government's Reply to the First Report of the Environment Committee on the Operation and Effectiveness of Part II of the Wildlife and Countryside Act 1981*, Cmnd. 9522 (HMSO, 1985).

There is nothing new about the use of such agreements; they have occasionally been employed in SSSIs in the past. What is new is the rate at which they are now being used as a result of the operation of Pt. II of the 1981 Act. The NCC *Annual Report* for the year ending March 31, 1987 states that 670 such agreements concerned with habitat protection covering 24,293 hectares were then in force. One hundred and forty-two of these agreements covering 14,241 hectares relate to SSSIs in Scotland. There is no doubt that the rate of uptake of these agreements makes them a significant force in controlling and guiding land use change in rural areas. It has been estimated that the annual cost to the NCC of such agreements for the whole of the United Kingdom in 1989–90 may be in excess of £18m.[14] The Government's own estimate is somewhat lower.[15]

(3) Compulsory agreements in SSSIs. There is one situation in which the NCC may be *required* to enter into an agreement. Section 32 of the Wildlife and Countryside Act 1981 provides that the Secretary of State must consider any objection from the NCC before reaching a decision on an application from a farmer of land in an SSSI for grant aid for agricultural improvement to his land under section 29 of the Agriculture Act 1970.

If such an application is refused because of an objection by the NCC based on the adverse effect which the improvements have had or will have on features of special scientific interest, then within three months of the Secretary of State's decision, the NCC must offer to enter into an agreement with the applicant. Such an agreement, may take the form of a nature reserve or SSSI agreement, as appropriate, imposing restrictions on the activities in question and providing for the payment of compensation (which will, it seems, reflect the profit foregone by the farmer).

This provision has been criticised as being likely to aggravate further the divide between agriculture and conservation in sensitive parts of the countryside. It also implies that a farmer has a right to grant aid, the denial of which is to be compensated, a position which many would regard as being unduly advantageous to the farmer. The Government's response to that is that "it would be rather unfair to put the particular farmer who happens to be in a conservation area at a disadvantage just because of that reason,

---

[14] L. Gould, *Consultant's Report on the Operation and Effectiveness of the Financial Guidelines for Management Agreements*, DoE, 1986.
[15] DoE, "Wildlife and Countryside Act 1981—review of Financial Guidelines", 1987.

as opposed to the farmer next door who might be getting the grant."[16]

6. Scenic and recreational agreements

(1) Countryside (Scotland) Act 1967, s. 49A.[17] The Countryside Commission for Scotland, in its report in 1974 entitled "A Park System for Scotland" drew attention to the role which could be played by management agreements between landowners and local authorities in tying recreational provision in with sound estate management.

A new section 49A has now been added to the Countryside (Scotland) Act 1967[18] which will enable planning authorities[19] and the Countryside Commission for Scotland to enter into management agreements with persons having an interest in land.

The purpose of such agreements will be to preserve or enhance the natural beauty of the countryside or to promote its enjoyment by the public. To achieve this, an agreement may provide for the doing of "whatever in the opinion of the parties may be necessary." Given the very general statement of purpose, this is a wide-ranging power and goes some way towards giving planning authorities a "general competence"[20] in countryside matters.

It is specifically provided that agreements may contain financial provisions and these provisions might cover both payments for works and compensation for restrictions. If properly recorded, agreements will be enforceable at the instance of the planning authority or the Commission against successors in title.

Examples of the sort of activities which management agreements might seek to promote or control are given in "A Study of Management Agreements" published in 1978 by the Countryside Commission for England. Any list must necessarily be open-ended but it could include obligations designed to mitigate the effects of

---

[16] W. Waldegrave, cited in the *First Report of the Environment Committee of the House of Commons on the Operation and Effectiveness of Part II of the Wildlife and Countryside Act* (HMSO, 1985).

[17] Added by the Countryside (Scotland) Act 1981, s. 9.

[18] Similar provision for England and Wales was made in the Wildlife and Countryside Act 1981, s. 39.

[19] General, regional and district planning authorities.

[20] The phrase is derived from the Royal Commission on Local Government in Scotland, Cmnd. 4150 (September, 1969), para. 640 and the Committee on the Management of Local Government (England and Wales) (HMSO, 1967), paras. 284–286, both of which recommended that local authorities should be given a general power to do whatever might be necessary to meet the needs of the community.

agricultural and forestry practices on the landscape, provisions designed to enhance nature conservation and the protection of historical sites, and the promotion of recreational facilities. To date, the Countryside Commission for Scotland have not used the power in section 49A and it is believed that only limited use has been made of such agreements by planning authorities.

To assist authorities, the Countryside Commission for Scotland have published a model form of management agreement together with explanatory notes.

(2) Compulsory management agreements. Section 41 of the Wildlife and Countryside Act 1981 provides that the Secretary of State must consider any objection from a planning authority[21] before reaching a decision on an application from a farmer of land in an area specified for the purposes of the section for grant aid for improvements to the land under section 29 of the Agriculture Act 1970.

If such an application is refused because of an objection by the planning authority based on the adverse effect which the improvements have had or will have on the natural beauty or amenity of the specified area or its enjoyment by the public then, within three months of the Secretary of State's decision, the authority must offer to enter into an agreement with the applicant. The agreement will take the form of a management agreement under section 49A of the Countryside (Scotland) Act 1967, imposing restrictions on the activities in question and providing for the payment of compensation which, it seems, will reflect the profit foregone by the farmer.

It will be apparent that this provision is in very similar terms to that which requires the NCC to enter into certain agreements in SSSIs and the same comments may be made. The effect of these provisions will depend very much on what areas are to be specified in Scotland for the purposes of this section and, as yet, there has been no indication from the Secretary of State.

(3) Access to the countryside. The preamble to the Countryside (Scotland) Act 1967 describes it as "an Act to make provision for the better enjoyment of the Scottish countryside." In view of the convention in Scotland which appears to allow the public much greater freedom of access to open land than in England and Wales, such legislation may at first sight seem unnecessary.

However, two reasons may be advanced for legislation in this

---

[21] The reference is to authorities exercising district planning functions.

area.[22] The first is that there may be inherent conflicts in some areas between recreational use and other more traditional uses. Secondly, access may be considerably enhanced, to the benefit of both the public and the landowner, by the provision of facilities such as information services, car parks, picnic areas, toilets, boat launching sites and by the introduction of a ranger service.

The 1967 Act[23] makes provision for access on an area basis to open country through the use of management agreements and on a linear basis by means of public path agreements and long-distance routes.

(a) *Access agreements.* Part II of the 1967 Act deals with access on an area basis to open country. "Open country" is defined as land comprised wholly or predominantly of: "mountain, moor, heath, hill, woodland, cliff or foreshore, with the waterways therein or contiguous or adjacent thereto and any waterway."[24] Planning authorities[25] have power to enter into agreements with any person having an interest in land for the purpose of securing access for the public to open country.[26] Two consequences follow from the existence of such an agreement. First of all, it entitles any member of the public to be on the land for open air recreation without running the risk of being treated as a trespasser. He may roam, if not at will, then at least within the terms of the agreement. Secondly, it prevents any persons with an interest in the land from doing anything which would have the effect of limiting the agreed level of access.

Access agreements may provide for the carrying out of works to provide safe and sufficient access, for the maintenance of these works, and for restrictions on the use and management of land which would impede access.[27] Persons with an interest in the land

---

[22] For a detailed discussion of the 1967 legislation see Francis Lyall, "Recreation, Land Ownership and the Countryside", 1970 J.R. 203; F. Lyall, "Access to the Countryside: Part II of the Countryside (Scotland) Act 1967"; 1969 S.L.T. (News) 197; and F. Lyall, "Access Through the Countryside: Part III of the Countryside (Scotland) Act 1967," 1969 S.L.T. (News) 205; also the Countryside Commission for Scotland, "Access to the Countryside", report of a one-day conference held on December 4, 1975.

[23] As amended in certain respects by the Countryside (Scotland) Act 1981.

[24] "Waterway" and "foreshore" are defined as including any bank, barrier, dune, beach, flat or other land adjacent to the waterway or foreshore (Countryside (Scotland) Act 1981, s. 2).

[25] General or district planning authorities (Local Government and Planning (Scotland) Act 1982, s. 9 and Sched. 1, para. 3).

[26] s. 13(1). Provision is also made for compulsory access orders (s. 14). It is thought that no such orders have been made in Scotland.

[27] For examples see M. Dobson, "Access Agreements in the Countryside" (1980) S.P.L.P. 12.

may be compensated both for the restrictions on use and for the costs, if any, incurred in carrying out any works. Agreements which are properly recorded may be enforced at the instance of the planning authority against successors in title. A revised model form of agreement, together with explanatory notes, has been prepared by the Countryside Commission for Scotland.

Planning authorities must maintain maps of land in their area covered by access agreements and these must be available for public inspection. There is no central register of such agreements but the Countryside Commission for Scotland believes that there may be between 30 and 40 in existence. Of these a number give formal recognition to areas of land which have already been popular for informal recreation. In Glen Nevis, for example, an area which is the subject of considerable recreational pressure, some 877 hectares of land are now covered by access agreements. Others form part of a larger plan for open-air recreation—for example, those which are to be found on long-distance walking routes.

Until the Countryside (Scotland) Act 1981 came into operation, access agreements were also used to provide "linear" footpath access thus enabling ranger service coverage of the footpaths subject to agreement. The 1981 Act now enables authorities to operate their ranger services on footpaths the subject of "public path creation agreements" (see *infra*).

The Secretary of State's consent is no longer required to enter into access agreements,[28] but we do not think that this will generate wider use of them in the next few years (unlike section 50 agreements—see Chapter 1). Indeed, the switch away from linear access agreements may well mean that less use is made of the power in section 13 of the 1967 Act.

(b) Linear access. Part III of the 1967 Act makes provision for two forms of linear access.

First of all, general or district planning authorities are given power to negotiate what are termed "public path creation agreements"[29] with any person having an interest in land. Such paths, which may be footpaths[30] or bridleways[31] enable the public to have

---

[28] Countryside (Scotland) Act 1981, s. 15 and Sched. 2.

[29] s. 30. Provision is also made for the compulsory creation of public paths (s. 31).

[30] "Footpath" is defined in s. 47 as "a way over which the public have the following, but no other, rights of way, that is to say, a right of way on foot with or without a right of way on pedal cycles."

[31] "Bridleway" is defined in s. 47 as "a way over which the public have the following, but no other, rights of way, that is to say, a right of way on foot and a right of way on horseback or leading a horse, with or without a right to drive animals of any description along that way."

access along a defined route by agreement rather than as of right.

Such agreements will provide for the creation of the path, for its maintenance and for compensation. If properly recorded, the agreement may be enforced at the instance of the authority against successors in title. It is not known how many public path creation agreements may have been concluded but the Countryside Commission for Scotland have noted a resurgence of interest in the use of such agreements following the provision in the Countryside (Scotland) Act 1981, which enables authorities to operate their ranger services on such paths.

The second form of linear access is the long-distance route. The initiative here rests with the Countryside Commission for Scotland. Where the Commission is of the opinion that there is a route which will enable the public to make extensive journeys on foot, bicycle or horseback, largely avoiding roads, then in consultation with planning authorities, it may prepare a scheme for submission to the Secretary of State.[32]

This scheme will incorporate a map and set out proposals for the provision, maintenance and enjoyment of the route. Amongst other things it may make suggestions for maintaining and improving existing public paths and roads, for the provision and maintenance of new paths, for the provision and operation of ferries and for accommodation, toilets, meals and refreshments. The scheme will include an estimate of capital outlay and annual expenditure. The Secretary of State may approve, modify, impose conditions on, or reject the scheme and will notify the Commission and the planning authorities of his decision.

It will then be for planning authorities along the route to implement the scheme through negotiation of access agreements and public path creation agreements. Other public bodies may also be able to contribute to the provision of the route. Should any part of the scheme turn out to be impracticable then revised proposals may be submitted to the Secretary of State for approval.

The first such long-distance route in Scotland, the West Highland Way, was opened in October 1980. This was followed by the Southern Upland Way which was opened in April 1984. The Speyside Way is currently being developed and a part was opened to the public in April 1981. Consideration is now being given to the development of a long-distance route through the Great Glen.[33]

---

[32] s. 39.
[33] *Countryside Commission for Scotland 19th Annual Report* (1986).

7. Environmentally Sensitive Area agreements

Where the Secretary of State for Scotland is of the opinion that the maintenance or adoption of particular agricultural methods is likely either: to conserve or enhance the natural beauty of an area; or to conserve the flora or fauna or geological or physiographical features of an area; or to protect buildings or other objects of archaeological, architectural or historic interest in the area he may designate the area as an "Environmentally Sensitive Area" (ESA) under section 18 of the Agriculture Act 1986. Such designations are made on the recommendation of the Countryside Commission for Scotland and the Nature Conservancy Council. The objective is to encourage farmers in such areas to continue with or to adopt farming methods which are environmentally benign. The scheme operates on a voluntary basis in the sense that there is no requirement for farmers to participate. However, some incentive to take part is provided in the form of payments to be made by the Department of Agriculture and Fisheries for Scotland (DAFS) in return for the management of the land in an agreed fashion.

Five ESAs have been designated so far in Scotland by the Secretary of State. These are:

Breadalbane;
Loch Lomond;
The Machair Lands of the Uists and Benbecula;
Whitelaw/Eildon; and
Stewartry.

Farmers participating in an ESA scheme are required to sign an agreement with DAFS in which they undertake to follow certain specified farming practices set out in a leaflet prepared by DAFS for each ESA entitled "Guidelines for Farmers." They are also obliged to prepare a farm conservation plan focusing on features of conservation interest and showing how the specified farming practices are to be put into effect.

"Farmers" for the purposes of sections 18 and 19 of the 1986 Act include all categories of persons with an interest in agricultural land. Tenant farmers must notify their landlord of an intention to take part in a scheme. Grazing committees may, with the consent of a majority of crofters in a township, enter into such an agreement in relation to any part of common grazings.

Land already designated as an NNR, an SSSI or a National Scenic Area may be brought into an ESA scheme but if a management agreement is already in existence with regard to the land, there will be no question of double funding.

Agreements are initially made for a period of five years and may be renewed thereafter. If recorded in the Register of Sasines or Land Register, as appropriate, such an agreement may be enforced at the instance of the Secretary of State against singular successors in title.

The consideration for undertaking to manage land in a specified way is in two parts. First of all, a flat rate payment is made based on the amount and type of land. This amounts to £15 p.a. for each hectare of enclosed land and £2.50 p.a. for each hectare of rough grazing with a maximum figure in respect of each individual farm business of £1,500 p.a. Special rates apply to farm businesses of less than 16 hectares. Secondly, additional payments are made, calculated on the basis of standard costings, in respect of specified farming operations identified in the farm conservation plan. Such additional payments are limited to a maximum of £3,000 per farm business or £100 p.a. per hectare whichever is the lower. Failure to implement the terms of an agreement may lead to its termination and to action to recover such payments.

It is too early to comment on the extent to which the designations are fulfilling their objective. A great deal will, of course, depend on the farmers' views of the adequacy of the flat rate payments.

Miscellaneous Agreements

8. Conservation agreements with the National Trust for Scotland

Paragraph 7 of the Schedule to the National Trust for Scotland Confirmation Act 1938 enables the Trust to enter into agreements with persons having an interest capable of binding land with a view to "restricting the planning, development or use of the land." The agreement may bind the land permanently or for a specified period and, if it is recorded in the Register of Sasines, it may be enforced by the Trust against successors in title.

The wording of paragraph 7 is very similar to that which was used in section 34 of the Town and Country Planning Act 1932. In *Ransom and Luck* v. *Surbiton Borough Council*[34] and in *Att. Gen.* v. *Barnes Corporation and Ranelagh Club*,[35] section 34 was held to be of limited application, merely enabling a planning authority to accept restrictions on land offered by a landowner. By analogy, paragraph 7 would appear to be "restrictive" of the use of land in the sense in which we define the term in Chapter 3.

---

[34] [1949] Ch. 180.
[35] [1939] Ch. 110.

It would seem that such agreements could not impose positive obligations on a proprietor of land.

Paragraph 7 requires that the conditions restricting the planning, development or use of land are to be in conformity with the purposes for which the Trust was established. The purposes are defined in the National Trust for Scotland Order Confirmation Acts of 1935 and 1938. These include the promotion, for the benefit of the nation, of the preservation of lands and buildings in Scotland of historic or national interest or natural beauty and of access to them by the public.

Considerable use has been made of such agreements in Scotland. The Trust uses them very much as a matter of course when it feus land or buildings, for example under its Little Houses Improvement Scheme. In this way it retains some control over proposed alterations. Over 600 such agreements have been concluded.

Apart from these, a number of agreements have been offered voluntarily by landowners and 53 of the main ones are listed in the Trust's *Year Book* for 1988. The Trust consults with the planning authority before concluding such agreements. In total, some 55,554 acres of land, virtually all of it in the countryside and including some 78 miles of coastline, are protected in this way. The increasing use of such agreements creates its own problems for the Trust which has only limited manpower available to carry out the necessary supervision.

Whilst it is open to the Trust to relax the application of a paragraph 7 agreement at the request of a landowner in any given case, it would seem that, in England at least where similar restrictions exist,[36] in the event of disagreement, a landowner could apply to the Lands Tribunal under section 84(1)(c) of the Law of Property Act 1925 to modify the agreement or lift it altogether.[37] For the reasons we have given in Chapter 7 we think it unlikely that similar application could competently be made to the Lands Tribunal for Scotland under section 1 of the Conveyancing and Feudal Reform (Scotland) Act 1970.

9. Forestry dedication agreements

The Forestry Act 1967, section 5, makes provision for proprietors of land to enter into agreements with the Forestry Commissioners dedicating the land for use for the growing of timber or other forest products. If recorded in the Register of Sasines, such

[36] See National Trust Act 1937, s. 8.
[37] See *Gee* v. *The National Trust for Places of Historic Interest or Natural Beauty* [1966] 1 W.L.R. 170.

agreements are enforceable at the instance of the Commissioners against successors in title. The incentive for landowners to dedicate land for forestry was the provision by the Commission of grants for planting and management.

The dedication arrangements varied over the years. With the Basis I Scheme the grant was calculated as a percentage of cost. With the Basis II Scheme the grant was assessed on a flat rate per hectare. In both cases, dedication was in perpetuity. Basis III was also assessed on a flat rate per hectare but dedication was generally for just one rotation. The Basis I Scheme was in fact rarely employed and owners of woodlands dedicated under Basis I or II could transfer to Basis III if they so desired.

As from July 1, 1981, Basis III has been closed to new applications and the Commission have switched to the Forestry Grant Scheme which simplifies the administrative and legal procedures and which entails no formal agreements.[38] Existing dedication agreements remain in force, although Basis III dedication is for one rotation only. Furthermore, when a dedicated estate changes hands, the successor in title is invited by the Commissioners to continue with the current approved "plan of operation" until the end of its five year term at which point the dedication will cease.[39] Forestry dedication agreements are, therefore, diminishing in number and will, in due course, disappear altogether.

10. The countryside and capital taxation relief

Provision is made for a rather different sort of agreement, but one which could conceivably have a noticeable effect on the use and management of land in the countryside, in the Capital Transfer Tax Act 1984 as amended by the Finance Act 1986.

In suitable cases, the Treasury may grant exemption from the payment of inheritance tax on the transfer of property, the exemption being conditional upon an undertaking by the proprietor to maintain and preserve the character of the property and to allow public access.[40] As the exemption is conditional upon the undertaking being implemented, enforcement is unlikely to prove problematic.

Suitable cases may include land of *outstanding* scenic, historic or scientific interest, buildings which should be preserved because

---

[38] *Forestry Commission 62nd Annual Report and Accounts 1981–82.*

[39] C. E. Hart, *Private Woodlands: A Guide to British Timber Prices and Forestry Costings* (published by the author, 1987).

[40] For a detailed explanation of these provisions see "Capital Taxation and the National Heritage" (H.M. Treasury, 1986).

of their *outstanding* historic or architectural interest and land adjoining such buildings which is essential for protecting the character and amenities of the buildings. The standards of scenic, historic, architectural or scientific interest are high and the Treasury will consult with the Nature Conservancy Council and the Countryside Commission and other bodies, but not apparently with planning authorities—at least directly—about the suitability of applications for exemption and about the management objectives and conditions to be incorporated into any such undertaking.

In correspondence with the Capital Taxes Office, we have been informed that, surprisingly, they have no statistics relating to the number of such agreements currently in existence in Scotland. It is difficult to see how any proper evaluation can be made of the effect of such agreements in the absence of this.

CHAPTER 10

THE ETHICS OF PLANNING GAIN

Introduction

IN Malcolm Grant's words:[1]

> "Planning agreements offer a flexible alternative to the more conventional forms of planning control, but there has been increasing concern in recent years about the abuse made of this flexibility by some authorities. Agreements may be used to impose obligations going well beyond those which may be sought through planning permissions and conditions, and to shield the deals from public scrutiny and external review. As the nature of the obligations imposed extends further and further away from the planning requirements of the particular development, it becomes difficult to resist the conclusion that the power is being used by the authority for an ulterior purpose usually the purpose of seeking the best possible 'price' for the planning permission being granted by them."

In an article which appeared in the *Journal of Planning and Environment Law*, Sir Desmond Heap and Anthony J. Ward declared:

> "The use (and misuse) of section 52 agreements . . . in the development control process is, these days, one of the most widely disputed and debated aspects of town planning law. It is a subject on which strong views are held, and rightly so, because it is the one area where there is a very real danger of the planning system being brought into disrepute."[2]

What Grant, Heap and Ward have in mind is the practice of bargaining for "planning gain" and much has been written on the reasons underlying that phenomenon, its extent and importance and the "ethics" of the practice.[3] The phrase "planning gain" can

---

[1] *Urban Planning Law*, p. 374.

[2] [1980] J.P.L. 631.

[3] See, *e.g.* Jeffrey Jowell, "Bargaining in Development Control" [1977] J.P.L. 414; Jeffrey Jowell. "The Limits of the Law in Urban Planning" [1977] C.L.P. 63; M. Grant, "Developers' Contributions and Planning Gains: Ethics and Legalities" [1978] J.P.L. 8; S. Byrne, "Conditions and Agreements: The Local Authority's Viewpoint" in *Development Control—Thirty Years On* (JPEL Occasional Paper, Sweet and Maxwell 1979); Sir D. Heap and A. J. Ward, "Planning Bargaining: the Pros and Cons" [1980] J.P.L. 631; J. Ratcliffe, "Planning Gain—

mean very different things to different people. One is reminded of Humpty Dumpty in *Through the Looking Glass*—"When *I* use a word," Humpty Dumpty said in rather a scornful tone, "it means just what I choose it to mean—neither more nor less." It may be that in one sense all planning agreements have some degree of "planning gain" or benefit as one of their objectives but what most people appear to have in mind when they talk of planning gain is some sort of benefit to the community which was not part of the original proposal by a developer, and was therefore negotiated, and is not of itself of any commercial advantage to the developer. There is, broadly, some attempt to extract a community benefit from the profits of a particular development. More narrowly, the Property Advisory Group (*infra*) defined planning gain as a benefit which could not validly be obtained by way of a condition on a planning permission. Department of the Environment circular 22/83 states that

> "'Planning gain' is a term which has come to be applied whenever, in connection with a grant of planning permission, a local planning authority seeks to impose on a developer an obligation to carry out works not included in the development for which permission has been sought or to make some payment or confer some extraneous right or benefit in return for permitting development to take place . . . In some cases the developer may offer some such works or payment in applying for planning permission or in the course of subsequent negotiations."

Grant states that there are major objections to planning agree-

---

An Overview" (1981) 258 E.G. 407; P. Boydell and S. Byrne, "Planning Gain: How is this Form of 'Plea Bargaining' Justified?" (Blundell Memorial Lecture, 1981); "Planning Gain." Report by the Property Advisory Group (HMSO, 1981); "Planning Gain". Comments by the RTPI on the Report by the Property Advisory Group, January, 1982; M. Grant, "False Diagnosis, Wrong Prescription," *Town and Country Planning*, March 1982; J. Jowell, "Giving Planning Gain a Bad Name," 1982 L.G.C. 155; E. J. Reade, "Section 52 and Corporatism in Planning" [1982] J.P.L. 8; A. J. Ward, "Planning Bargaining: Where do we Stand?" [1982] J.P.L. 74; "Planning Gain: The Law Society's Observations" [1982] J.P.L. 346; M. Loughlin, "Planning Gain: Another Viewpoint" [1982] J.P.L. 352; J. Jowell and M. Grant, "Guidelines for Planning Gain?" [1983] J.P.L. 427; J. Jowell and M. Grant, "A Critical Look at Planning Gain" (1983) 147 L.G.R. 427; I. Simpson, "Planning Gain" in M. L. Harrison and R. Mordey (eds.), *Planning Control: Philosophies, Prospects and Practice* (Croom Helm, 1987); Royal Town Planning Institute "Planning Gain Guidelines," (Observations submitted to the Department of the Environment, April 1983); R. W. Spinney "Planning Gain—A Developer's Viewpoint" in *Contemporary Planning Policies* (JPEL Occasional Paper, Sweet and Maxwell, 1984); M. Grant, *Urban Planning Law* (Sweet and Maxwell, 1982, 1st Supplement, 1986), pp. 374–377.

ments and that these concern in the main planning gain. He says that there is the fear

> "that authorities may have engaged in the sale of planning permission, prescribing conditions of little relevance to the proposed development but of great financial benefit to the authority. There is the fact that the developer's willingness to agree to onerous terms is likely to be greatest in circumstances where planning controls are most rigid; not simply because of a realisation that something substantial might be needed to induce the authority to relax their policies, but because of the vast potential difference between the value of the land with no permission and no apparent prospect of it, and its value with permission for development. This *quid pro quo* approach to planning may lead to thoroughly bad development, because the less likely the prospect of permission under established plans and policies, the greater the increment in land value if permission is actually granted . . . Planning control and development profit are uneasy partners."[4]

Planning gain of various types may be sought by planning authorities by way of a planning agreement. In the south east of England in particular, where planning gain appears to be much more commonly sought (and obtained) than in Scotland, substantial gains are, it seems, frequently achieved by planning authorities.[5] It is apparently common, for example, for authorities to seek the provision of a certain amount of residential accommodation in a proposed office development, or to require a developer to carry out or pay for the widening of a public highway serving the development site, or to have a developer reserve land on a housing estate for shops or a school.

Many of the Scottish agreements we have seen do not really involve planning gain in any of the usual senses of that phrase. Many of the agreements are concerned with perfectly normal development control matters such as landscaping or restrictions on use. Planning gain is not the objective of these agreements; rather, their purpose is to allow the planning authority to impose, for example, tighter controls than would be possible by means of ordinary development control powers or to make it simpler for the authority to take enforcement action.

However, though planning gain is less commonly sought (or is perhaps much less easily obtainable[6]) in Scotland than would

---

[4] *Urban Planning Law*, p. 359.

[5] For accounts of some English agreements under which gain was sought see, in particular, J. Jowell, "Bargaining in Development Control" [1977] J.P.L. 414; and R. W. Spinney, "Planning Gain—A Developer's Viewpoint" in *Contemporary Planning Policies* (JPEL Occasional Paper, Sweet and Maxwell, 1984).

[6] This may well be because it is generally only in areas of high land values that a

appear to be the case in England, the use of planning agreements to obtain planning gain appears to be increasing in Scotland. In Scotland agreements have, for example, been used to have retail developers make provision for industrial floor space or sport or leisure facilities, or to make provision for public use of private car parks. Agreements have also made provision for a gift of land by a developer for a country park; to ensure reinstatement of land used for opencast coal mining to a higher standard than it was originally; to secure the provision of public open space outwith but adjoining the site of a development; to obtain public walkways over land; to secure the extinguishment of uses situated in inappropriate locations; to have developers provide public parking; to require a developer of retail premises to make over part of the site for industrial purposes; and to require a developer to lay out land in a housing estate for public open space and to make provision for its future maintenance (see *supra*). On occasion the developer himself will, in order to make a proposed development more attractive to the planning authority or to overcome some possible obstacle to a development, make an offer of some collateral benefit to the planning authority.

In the main the "ethical" arguments about planning by agreement relate to bargaining for planning gain. Planning gain is an emotive and divisive subject. As the *Estates Gazette* said:

> "On the one hand it can be represented as no more than the justifiable gathering by the local community of a small proportion of the increment inseparable from the granting of planning permission. At the other extreme it can be seen by some local authorities as a passport to a range of highly desirable benefits only tenuously connected with the development in question."[7]

Of all the problems relating to planning by agreement the "ethical" problems are perhaps the most intractable. Some of the main arguments are summarised below.[8]

For and against planning gain

It is very difficult to determine where the line should be drawn as to the acceptable limits of planning gain; some would go so far as to argue that there is no place for it in the planning system. It is often said that there is an element of covert, if not overt, coercion in many agreements. There is a threat—either stated or

---

commerical developer will be able to negotiate over or to offer some planning gain.

[7] (1982) 262 E.G. 114.

[8] The detailed arguments are well made in many of the publications listed in n. 3 above.

implied—that if the developer does not enter into an agreement which satisfies the planning authority, planning permission will be refused. The developer's only alternative is to appeal to the Secretary of State, with all the expense and delay that that necessarily involves. Words such as blackmail are frequently used.

Assuming, however, that the planning authority would have reasonable planning grounds for refusing planning permission and that the planning objections can be overcome by agreement, such a "threat" by the planning authority does not seem improper. Where perhaps the "threat" does become improper is if it is used merely to extract some additional benefit from a development which is perfectly acceptable and would normally receive planning permission. The Sheaf Committee on public sector/private enterprise partnership schemes considered, for example that it would be a cogent objection to planning bargaining if a planning authority were to seek to obtain infrastructure gain in cases where land was already ripe and suitable for development.

Grant states that: "As the nature of the obligations imposed extends further and further away from the planning requirements of the particular development, it becomes difficult to resist the conclusion that the power is being used by the authority for an ulterior purpose—usually the purpose of securing the best possible 'price' for the planning permission being granted by them."[9]

The planning authority will sometimes be in a position to exercise pressure on a developer. There is, however, another side to the coin. A developer may offer a benefit which is difficult for the planning authority to resist—a benefit which is regarded by the planning authority as an important planning gain and is seen by the local population as a very considerable benefit to the area. Boydell cites the example of a company with a chain of superstores which applied for planning permission to build a big store near the centre of a town. The proposed floorspace was generous in relation to the shopping needs of the town. However, the company also offered to build, on land adjacent to the proposed superstore, a complex of indoor bowling greens and to give the complex to the town. This offer was not only regarded by the planning authority as an important planning gain but at the ensuing public inquiry (the application having been called in by the Secretary of State) it was clear that the proposal was supported by a wide section of the population.[10]

---

[9] *Urban Planning Law*, p. 374.
[10] See "Planning Gain: How is this Form of 'Plea Bargaining' Justified?" (Blundell Memorial Lecture, 1981), p. 11.

It is said that planning authorities are sometimes prepared to relax normal planning standards to an unacceptable degree or even to abandon established planning policies in exchange for some planning gain. The decision in such a case may be made less on planning than on financial grounds. Sometimes, it is claimed, authorities waive a planning objection in exchange for some gain which has no connection with the particular development or with specific objections to it. Why, it is asked, should a proposal to build an office block receive favourable consideration just because the developer is also prepared to offer to build the authority a sports centre?

Planning authorities, with the "carrot" of planning gain dangled before them, may be tempted to take too short term a view of particular proposals. If, for example, there is a present shortage of housing, then an immediate housing gain may seem to be of greater value than the loss of a single site to unsatisfactory development. However, the equation between planning loss and planning gain may look rather different over the longer term.

Where some contribution is required from a developer—e.g. new roads, improved sewers, play facilities, etc.—it may be that a distinction should be drawn between facilities or infrastructure reasonably required as a result of the developer's proposals and those not so required. It is difficult to see much objection to the former sort of requirement but it is much harder to justify a requirement to provide infrastructure or buildings which have no connection with the developer's proposals. Heap and Ward concede, for example, that it may be reasonable for a planning authority to ask a developer to spend money restoring a listed building standing on the development site but it is, in their view, an "abuse of discretion" for an authority to refuse to grant permission for an otherwise unobjectionable scheme of office development until the developer has agreed to spend money on someone else's listed building at the other end of the borough.[11] If a planning decision is influenced by some extraneous benefit offered by the developer, the authority could be accused of simply selling planning permission and if a developer is coerced into providing such extraneous benefits allegations of blackmail can be made—in forcing a developer to provide something in excess of what is required to cater for his proposed development, the

---

[11] [1980] J.P.L. 632. See also S. Byrne in "Planning Gain: How is this Form of 'Plea Bargaining' Justified?" (Blundell Memorial Lecture, 1981). There might be some doubt about the legality of such a requirement.

authority might be said to be using its position to extract improper benefits from the developer.

Spinney disagrees with the argument that planning gain plays a part in raising the standard of development. In his view improving the quality of development can best be achieved by good planning control, by market forces and by a greater interest in commercial architecture by members of the architectural and planning professions, many of whose members have not been prepared to be associated with commercial developments. He states that as market forces dictate the price that can be charged—and therefore the value—then the price payable for the raw material, the land, must be reduced to meet the cost of planning gain. The individual who is therefore disadvantaged by the imposition of planning gain requirements is the landowner rather than the developer. The developer is not as concerned as the landowner if the development value is reduced so long as it does not unduly restrict the supply of land. Spinney also says that the principal leverage available to a planning authority in the bargaining process is delay. Appeals take a long time, may not be successful and may prejudice financial arrangements.[12]

Although the subject-matter of many agreements involving planning gain will often be of general public interest—as involving, for example, relaxation of normal planning standards—little publi‑ city is likely to be given to the negotiations concerning the gain until the matter comes before the planning committee.[13] Members of the authority are likely to be presented by their officials with a virtually completed package—almost a fait accompli—and members of the public may have no opportunity to comment on or to criticise the arrangements. Such secrecy in decision-making by public authorities may be thought to exclude an important control over discretion in that it is much more difficult to override legitimate interests in an atmosphere of openness.

The practice of bargaining for planning gain is to a large extent opportunistic. It may be ad hoc, arbitrary and unpredictable. As Jowell points out,[14] a feature of bargaining is "the abandonment of the legal value of 'evenhanded justice,' of like cases being treated alike." As he also points out, there is "an absence in the bargaining process of controls aimed to avoid illegality, corruption

---

[12] R. W. Spinney, "Planning Gain—A Developer's Viewpoint" in *Contemporary Planning Policies* (JPEL Occasional Paper, Sweet and Maxwell, 1984). See also J. Rowan-Robinson and M. G. Lloyd, *Land Development and the Infrastructure Lottery* (T. & T. Clark, Edinburgh, 1988), Chap. 6.
[13] See "Planning Gain: the Law Society's Observations" [1982] J.P.L. 350.
[14] [1977] J.P.L. 414.

and the abuse of the considerable discretion allocated to planning authorities with the powers in development control."

The Sheaf Committee recommended that agreements should be used in order to allow the bringing forward of development which would otherwise be premature because of infrastructure problems. It has been argued, however, that the use of agreements in this way can give an unfair advantage to the larger and wealthier developer who is able to finance the initial investment in infrastructure.

Whatever objections may be made to the practice of planning bargaining, there are probably many developers and planning authorities who would wish the practice to continue. For the developer it ensures speed, certainty and commitment on the part of the planning authority. For the planning authority agreements add an element of flexibility to the development control process. Instead of simply reacting to market forces, the authority may be able to achieve a degree of positive planning and to secure the implementation of policies which might not otherwise be feasible. The planning authority may also be able to secure for the local community some benefit it would not otherwise have had.

Often, therefore, both sides will feel they have something to gain by way of an agreement. Planning by agreement means that each side achieves at least some of its objectives and avoids conflict. It also means that both sides avoid the possibility of total loss: this is what Jowell calls the "minimax principle"—negotiation and agreement minimise the risk of maximal loss.[15]

Some planning authorities see it as part of their function to seek the return of part of the developer's profit to the community (by whom the profit is created) in the form of planning gain. Town planning is thus, in effect, being used as a redistributive mechanism. Against this approach, it can be argued that taxation of development gains is the prerogative of central government and of general legislation. Heap and Ward declare[16] that: the "system [of planning by agreement] was not designed, nor is it suitable, for achieving the ulterior objective of sharing out the development profits in land."

It has, however, been argued by some that legislation should provide for the overt sale of planning permissions. Graham Mather argues,[17] for example, that town planning is in need of a thorough

---

[15] [1977] C.L.P. 63.
[16] [1980] J.P.L. 631. See also "Planning Gain," the Report of the Property Advisory Group (*infra*).
[17] "Pricing for Planning," IEA Inquiry No. 3 (Institute of Economic Affairs, 1988).

overhaul, the system being incapable of handling the economic consequences of development effectively. He says that notwithstanding central government aims to operate the planning system to facilitate development and renewal, local authorities face strong political pressure from existing residents to restrict housing and commercial development. The market has begun to provide a solution to the problem with local authorities attaching an effective "price"—in the form of "planning gain"—to the grant of planning consents. Developers are invited to provide infrastructure improvements, finance road schemes and build health and community centres and other facilities.

Mather considers that in addition to attaching a "price" to the grant of planning consents, the planning gain system could compensate local residents for the short-term disadvantages of developments by allowing environmental improvements to be secured. The system is, however, informal and the cause of tension between central and local government. Formalising it by allowing local authorities to sell or auction planning consents could provide an incentive to grant permission for development on land currently blighted; rank the authority's criteria for development and allow a clearer indication of priorities; pass to the community a sum which would "compensate" for apparent detriment; and maximise the use of the least environmentally important land. The proposed system of pricing would place on a formal footing the informal and sometimes shadowy workings of planning gain. There are undoubted problems with planning gain but, as an *Estates Gazette* editorial[18] asked, "is the whole loose system so open to abuse that it needs to be replaced by something far more structured?" The editorial continued: "In the event, this very flexibility may be a major advantage, for successful schemes now hinge largely on public and private sector partnerships arrived at through bargaining." Mather considers, however, that the "introduction of pricing for a wider range of planning decisions" was to be preferred to the present hotchpotch.

The Report of the Property Advisory Group

In 1980 the Property Advisory Group, appointed by the Secretary of State for the Environment, was asked to report on the "problem" of planning gain. Their report, "Planning Gain", was published in 1981. The report was very critical of the practice, apparently flourishing south of the border, of bargaining for planning gain.

---

[18] 8814 E.G. 1.

For the purpose of the report the Group took the view that a planning gain accrued when, in connection with the obtaining of a planning permission, a developer offered, agreed or was obliged to incur some expenditure, surrender some right or concede some other benefit which could not, or arguably could not, be embodied in a valid planning condition. This definition excludes those cases in which, although the planning authority could impose a valid planning condition, it prefers for reasons of more effective enforcement, or ease of drafting, to enter into an agreement with the developer to the like effect, or to invite the developer to submit a revised application. The definition also excludes cases where the agreement is a genuine alternative to a valid condition.

The Property Advisory Group conceded that planning gain has many powerful advocates and that there were numerous examples of developers who had freely and willingly conferred upon the local community various sorts of services, amenities and benefits which the community would not otherwise have enjoyed. Subject to two exceptions, however, they were unable to accept that planning gain had any place in the town planning system, their main objection being that if decisions on the planning merits of a development proposal were generally to be linked to the willingness of developers to offer extraneous or collateral benefits the whole planning system would become distorted and fall into disrepute.

In the Group's view planning gain could only be justified in two sets of circumstances:

(1) If the purpose of the agreement was to overcome what might be a legitimate ground for refusing planning permission altogether but which, for some technical legal reason, could not form, or arguably might not form, the subject-matter of a valid planning condition. The examples given of this sort of gain were the provision, off the development site itself, of necessary infrastructure or public services.

(2) If the application was for a "mixed" development containing several different elements, some of which, taken in isolation, would be objectionable but others of which would promote positive planning objectives. As examples the report cited development in the green belt coupled with a sports centre, and the change of use of a listed building coupled with restoration or repair. In such a situation it might, the Group considered, be legitimate for the planning authority to grant planning permission if satisfied that the proposed advantages outweighed the disadvantages.

As Jeffrey Jowell pointed out[19] many agreements providing for

---

[19] 1982 L.G.C. 155.

planning gain are covered by this second exception and a large swathe is thus cut through the Group's general condemnation of planning gain.

Some development plans and policy documents make provision for planning gain which did not satisfy the Group's criteria of acceptability. In the Group's view such plans should be reconsidered. It was, they said, "plain that if a practice is wrong you cannot make it right by setting it out in print in a public document which becomes converted into public policy." Malcolm Grant commented on this: "Not so. Whether a policy is good or bad, its inclusion in a statutory plan renders it a 'material consideration' in development control, so far as it is material to the application being determined. The policy is then legally 'right', and failure to have regard to it may invalidate the decision."[20]

The Property Advisory Group agreed that some form of central guidance on planning gain was necessary for the benefit of all interested parties.[21] Such guidance, they said, could only come from the Secretary of State but they did not think it necessary to go so far as to draw up an elaborate code of practice. The Group suggested the following guidelines:

(1) When a local authority received an application for planning permission, it should be considered on its own merits, and as a whole.

(2) If the proposal was one to which no legitimate planning objection could be raised, the authority should grant permission.

(3) If there were objections to the proposal which could be overcome by the imposition of valid planning conditions, permission should be granted subject to those conditions.

(4) If there were objections to the proposal which, but for some technical legal objection, could be overcome by the imposition of a valid planning condition, the local authority should be willing to grant planning permission subject to the developer's entering into an agreement under section 52 of the 1971 Act or other powers which would overcome the legitimate planning objection.

---

[20] *Town and Country Planning*, March 1982, p. 59.

[21] Several bodies and individuals have argued for some form of guidance on the acceptable limits of planning gain. See, for example, the RTPI's comments on the Property Advisory Group Report and "Planning Gain: The Law Society's Observations" [1982] J.P.L. 346. According to Heap and Ward, "nothing is more certain than that some local planning authorities, whether they realise it or not, are desperately in need of reliable guidance." ([1980] J.P.L. 631). It might be asked, however, whether the use of planning agreements is likely to be brought under control by a mere policy statement from central government; planning by agreement is almost entirely outside the purview of central government.

(5) If the application was a "mixed" application which contained a number of elements, some of which were, by themselves, objectionable, but others of which promoted positive planning advantages, the separate elements should be looked at individually as well as collectively so that, in the final result, the decision on the application, which must be a decision on the application as a whole, would achieve a just balance which could not be characterised as the mere "sale" of development rights.

The practice of seeking contributions from developers towards the cost of providing car-parking spaces should, they thought, be governed by the same principles.

The Group concluded that subject to the exceptions mentioned above, "the practice of bargaining for planning gain is unacceptable and should be firmly discouraged." They do not, however, specify how this is to be done.

Views of the Property Advisory Group Report

The report was heavily criticised.[22] It was described, for example, by Malcolm Grant as a report "which takes a remarkably narrow view of a complex phenomenon, which side-steps many of the essential economic and legal issues and which then dares to attempt a general prescription based only on the particular symptoms identified by the group."[23]

Loughlin points out[24] that "the procedural dimension to the planning gain controversy is almost entirely ignored" in the report; he states: "the issue of principle cannot properly be dealt with without examining the procedures and mechanisms used for negotiating and obtaining planning gain." The question of statutory powers is also largely ignored, except that it is stated that "planning gain represents an ad hoc local tax not authorised by Parliament." Ministers have, however, accepted that the present statutory powers allow planning authorities to obtain planning gain. There is no consideration of such questions as whether statute should provide for regulation of procedures, whether it should provide an opportunity to appeal from an agreement or for arbitration on an agreement, or whether it should in some way provide for public challenge of an agreement.

---

[22] See, in particular, M. Grant, "False Diagnosis, Wrong Prescription," *Town and Country Planning*, March 1982; J. Jowell, "Giving Planning Gain a Bad Name," 1982 L.G.C. 155; M. Loughlin, "Planning Gain: Another Viewpoint" [1982] J.P.L. 352. However, the [English] Law Society's Standing Committee on Planning Law broadly accepted the Property Advisory Group's conclusions (see [1982] J.P.L. 346).

[23] See n. 22 *supra*.

[24] See n. 22 *supra*.

The report spoke of planning authorities seeking to obtain from developers "benefits collateral to the scheme in question in circumstances of doubtful legality", but there was no real consideration of the difficult questions that arise as to the exact limits of the statutory powers. Nor, as Jowell pointed out[25], were the specific dangers of planning gain—relating in the main to possible abuse of discretion and the matter of public accountability—dealt with in the report. Jowell declared that the control procedures which might help to solve these problems were not even hinted at.

Grant[26] makes a plea for a "more competent and comprehensive analysis of the problem." He states:

> "A study which examined the economic forces behind planning gain might conclude instead that an effective development land tax with direct or indirect distribution of the proceeds might serve to reduce the pressures: while a study of the administration of development control might conclude that rules should be devised to bring planning gain out of the closet and encourage public participation and the publication of specific criteria intended for even-handed application."

Grant concedes that crude planning gain may undermine firm planning restrictions, and that there is a need for reform. But it must, he says, "be reform which goes to the cause of the malaise, and is not confined merely to frowning on its symptoms."

Categorisation of various types of planning gain as legitimate and others as improper in the manner adopted by the Property Advisory Group seems to be of very limited usefulness. So much depends on the circumstances of the individual agreement and on one's views of the proper limits of town and country planning that it seems almost impossible to devise any satisfactory general test.[27] In Jowell's words:[28] "There is surely no precise point where planning gain becomes wrong per se. Like so much else in planning law and practice, it is a matter of fact and degree." Perhaps a more useful approach would have been to attempt to indicate the unacceptable features of planning gain.

The Property Advisory Group's main objection to planning gain was that "as soon as a system of accepting public benefits is established which goes beyond the strict consideration of the

---

[25] See n. 22 *supra.*
[26] See n. 22 *supra.*
[27] Various formulae for determining the propriety or otherwise of planning gain are considered in detail by Martin Loughlin in "Planning Gain: Law, Policy and Practice" (1981) 1 Oxford Jo. of Legal Studies 61.
[28] See n. 22 *supra.*

planning merits of a proposed development, the entire system of development control becomes subtly distorted and may fall into disrepute." This, and the Group's use of phrases such as "legitimate planning objection" and "extraneous benefit" indicate, as Grant says,[29] that the Group's

> "perception of development control is apparently that of a process of interpreting and applying clear cut rules to planning applications, as if it were a narrow technical type of operation. Their apparent lack of understanding of the political (in the broadest sense) context of decision-making, and the difficult choices it often poses between objectionable development and, for example, job retention or creation, leads them too readily to characterise planning gain as an extraneous element in a straightforward and narrowly conceived yes/no choice, rather than a potentially critical element in a complex evaluative process."

The narrowness of the report's approach was also criticised by the London Boroughs Association which said in a report to the Secretary of State for the Environment that the Property Advisory Group Report "fails to acknowledge a wider role for planning than merely its negative controlling mechanism."[30] It is perhaps the question of the proper scope of planning, and of development control in particular, that is at the heart of the controversy about planning gain.

In their comments[31] on the Property Advisory Group Report the Royal Town Planning Institute agreed with the Group that planning gain should never lead to an unacceptable development being given planning permission. However, in their comments the RTPI made a strong case for planning gain and stated that they believed that substantial restrictions upon the power to seek planning gain would have the undesirable consequences of more refusals of planning permission and, if adequate land were to be available and serviced for development, a consequential need for greater use of compulsory purchase powers and public sector funds.

The RTPI believed that there was a need to reduce the delays to which negotiations over agreements could give rise. They considered that the planning system should move as quickly as possible to a position where planning authorities would not normally seek planning gain which was not mentioned in a development plan or a development brief. This would reduce

---

[29] See n. 20 *supra*.
[30] See (1981) 261 E.G. 614.
[31] January, 1982.

uncertainty, distortion, arbitrariness and the number of appeals. It would also meet the suggestion made by the RICS that planning gain requirements should be reasonable and predictable.

The RTPI considered that in order to assist authorities to establish policies on planning gain requirements, the professional institutions concerned, in consultations with the government, should draw up an advice note covering such matters as contributions to off-site sewerage and road works, land or buildings for community uses, measures to ameliorate necessary but locally undesirable development, and the revocation of permission or the giving up of existing use rights in exchange for a new permission.

Once such policies and practical advice on planning gain had been established it would be open to the local ombudsman to investigate cases in which policy or advice had not been followed. In this way unreasonable practices and unnecessary delay would be discouraged.

Further, the RTPI considered that in a case where the sole reason for refusal of planning permission was the unwillingness of a developer to agree to provide a planning gain which is subsequently found by an inspector on appeal to be unreasonable or inappropriate, the costs of the appeal should be awarded against the planning authority.

Finally, the RTPI made the comment that some of the difficulties which arose in negotiating planning gain would be reduced if there were to be a substantial re-casting of planning and financial legislation.

Central government advice—England and Wales

In 1983 the Department of the Environment issued a consultation paper on the subject of planning gain. These draft guidelines showed very much less antipathy towards the concept of planning gain than had the Property Advisory Group Report. The guidelines defined "planning gain" in a way which could embrace conditions attached to planning permissions as well as planning agreements.

The Royal Town Planning Institute described the guidelines as "a useful first step but limited and too restrictive." The Institute were concerned that the draft said nothing of "the positive role of planning authorities in shaping the development of their area, or of the need for positive proposals and policies to be contained within development plans and policy statements." Nor was there any reference to "the positive role of developers and the many excellent developments achieved by effective co-operation and agreements over the years." The definition of "planning gain" was so wide that it implied that any requirements or obligations in connection with a permission was a "gain" even if the application might have been woefully deficient in material matters.

The RTPI considered that obligations sought to be imposed on a developer could fall into one of three classes:

1. Requirements to meet basic planning standards:
2. Excessive or totally unrelated demands for benefits:
3. An area in between, where legitimate related benefits or improvements to the scheme could be sought and agreed between the parties as good planning practice.

The first could not be described as "gain", the second was not acceptable and resulted in distortion of the proper planning process, and only the third could be considered legitimate planning gain. The third situation could be defined as one where a developer incurred some additional liability in providing a benefit he would not otherwise have chosen to provide but which the local planning authority have justifiable grounds for seeking to achieve. This is not, of course, an objective test but it may be that no test that is entirely objective can be found to measure the propriety of planning gains.

In an article[32] mainly concerned with the draft guidelines Jowell and Grant posed the question "How should planning gain be controlled?" They argued that the rise of planning gain came about for a large number of reasons. These included the removal of the need for ministerial consent to agreements, the move towards a style of development control based more on negotiation than regulatory adjudication which was identified in and grew from the Sheaf Committee's review of public sector/private enterprise partnership schemes, the increasing delays in determining planning appeals, and the Community Land Act 1975 which was founded on a negotiated system of control.

They suggested that the main defects of the DoE's draft guidelines were that they were based on the assumption that purely administrative guidance to local authorities would suffice to deflate planning gain, without any consideration of the mix of economic and administrative factors, some of them mentioned above, that encouraged it. The tests for the propriety of agreements suggested in the draft guidelines matched very closely the tests for the validity of planning conditions. However, Jowell and Grant pointed out that the reason for using agreements may well be to escape the legal restrictions on conditions. They said:

"Planning gain raises a fundamental challenge to a regulatory system

---

[32] "A Critical Look at Planning Gain" (1983) 147 L.G.R. 491.

of planning, and it is wishful thinking to assume that the guidelines will succeed in pushing it aside. Too little is known about planning gain, its incidence, its effects, who pays for it, what forces shape it, what alternatives there are or how it could be brought under control."

In August 1983 the DoE issued circular 22/83, entitled "Planning Gain." The circular provides guidance for local planning authorities in England and Wales on planning gain and sets out criteria intended to establish whether or not planning gain can reasonably be sought from a developer. Circular 22/83's advice on planning gain is broadly similar to that contained in SDD Circular 22/1984 (*infra*).

The RTPI described the circular as "helpful," though they noted that little was said in the document on the role of planning authorities in shaping development and achieving positive improvements in their areas. The Institute also considered that there was insufficient emphasis on what it termed "the successes already recorded in many excellent examples of willing co-operation between planning authorities and developers." The RTPI recommended the promulgation of a code of practice "agreed by government and the relevant professions to avoid distortion of planning decisions by inducements from developers or by unreasonable demands by planning authorities."

Central government advice—Scotland

In August 1984 the Scottish Development Department issued SDD Circular 22/1984 entitled "Section 50 Agreements." Unlike DoE circular 22/1983 (*supra*) the Scottish circular does not attempt to define planning gain. In other respects it is, however, broadly similar to the English circular. A copy of the circular appears as Appendix 2.

The Scottish circular advises planning authorities that planning applications should only be refused when this serves a clear planning purpose. The question of imposing a condition or obligation should arise only where it is considered that it would not be appropriate to grant planning permission in the terms sought— *i.e.* without the condition or obligation. While a planning authority might wish to attach a particular obligation to a grant of planning permission, not all desirable obligations can be imposed by way of a condition. The circular cites the following examples:

"(a) because a valid or effective planning condition cannot be imposed, eg to require works to be carried out on land not included in the site of the development for which planning permission has been requested although an assurance that such works will be carried out would be essential before planning permission could be granted; or

(b) because of the adverse effects that the proposed development would have on the surrounding area which could be overcome only by the carrying out by public or private bodies of infrastructure works such as road improvement schemes or additional car parking provision, but which may not be undertaken by these bodies because of financial constraints or competing priorities; or

(c) because a condition required in any grant of planning permission would not be capable of enforcement against successors in title of the developers; or

(d) because the proposed development would be incompatible with an existing grant of planning permission for a development on an adjacent site."

Rather than refuse planning permission in such circumstances, the circular suggests that a section 50 agreement may enable the development to proceed. The circular provides that:

"Where a condition would be difficult to enforce in practice or inadequate or inappropriate, an agreement under section 50 freely entered into may be appropriate to enable the original development to proceed. In some cases the developer may offer to carry out some works or make some payment either when applying for planning permission or in the course of subsequent negotiations with the planning authority in order to overcome a difficulty in securing the grant of planning permission. The guidance in this circular is relevant to those circumstances as well as to cases where the authority take the initiative."

An authority should not, says the circular, seek to treat the applicant's need for permission as an opportunity to obtain some extraneous benefit or advantage or as an opportunity to exact a payment for the benefit of the ratepayers at large. Nor should the preparation of such an agreement be permitted to delay unduly the decision on the application. A set of tests of reasonableness is set out in the circular. The question whether it would be reasonable to impose an obligation on a developer depends substantially on whether what is required:

"(1) is needed to enable the development to go ahead, eg provision of adequate access, water supply and sewerage and sewage disposal facilities; or

(2) in case of financial payments, will contribute to meeting the cost of providing such facilities in the near future; or

(3) is otherwise so directly related to the proposed development and to the use of the land after its completion that the

development ought not to be permitted without it, eg the
provision, whether by the developer or by the authority at the
developer's expense, of car parking in or near the development
or reasonable amounts of open space related to the development;
or

(4) is designed in the case of mixed development to secure an
acceptable balance of uses."

If what is required or sought passes one of the tests set out above,
a further test has to be applied. This is whether the extent of what
is required or sought is fairly and reasonably related in scale and
kind to the proposed development. Thus, while the developer
might reasonably be expected to pay for or contribute to the cost
of infrastructure which would not have been necessary but for his
development and while some public benefit might eventually
accrue from this, his payments should be directly related in scale
and kind to the benefit which the proposed development will
derive from the facilities to be provided.

There is also a final test,

"namely whether what the developer is being asked to provide or
help to finance represents in itself a reasonable charge on the
developer as distinct from being financed by national or local taxation
or other means—eg as a charge on those using the facility provided.
The essential principle to apply is that the facility to be provided or
financed should be directly related to the development in question
or the use of the land after development. It would not normally be
reasonable, for example, to seek a contribution to road construction or
improvement in the immediate vicinity of the proposed development
unless the need for this arises wholly or substantially from the new
development."

The criterion of reasonableness, used throughout the circular
makes it difficult to judge what can be required of a developer in an
agreement, and as Grant points out,[33] reliance on reasonableness is
not of much value where a developer volunteers a planning gain,
since the only remedy available where an obligation is considered
unreasonable by a developer is appeal to the Secretary of State.
The criterion may also require review in light of the decision in
R. v. Gillingham Borough Council, ex p. F. Parham Ltd.[34] (see
infra and Chapter 5).

The circular points out that where a developer provides open
space or other facilities such as amenity walkways he cannot be
required to dedicate these to the public (though he may volunteer

---

[33] *Urban Planning Law* (1st Supplement), p. 374.
[34] [1988] J.P.L. 336.

such an arrangement). If authorities consider that general public access is appropriate, and the developer does not wish to provide it, it is for authorities to seek acquisition of the necessary rights in the land.

The circular also raises the question whether

"in addition to providing facilities such as open space or contributing to their capital costs, developers should also be expected to pay towards their maintenance costs. Where such facilities are of general public benefit the developer may be willing to dedicate them to the public. In such cases the developer's responsibility should be limited to providing what is needed in the first instance and all costs of subsequent maintenance should normally be borne by the authority or body in which the asset is to be vested. However, in smaller scale developments, such as housing estates, open areas of grass or landscaping are principally of benefit to the development itself rather than to the wider public and the developer can reasonably be expected to make suitable provision for subsequent maintenance. This may not be a matter which can be dealt with effectively by means of a planning condition. In appropriate circumstances, authorities may, therefore, wish to discuss the issue with prospective developers with a view to securing an agreement on maintenance arrangements. Such an agreement might, for instance, provide for a suitable commuted maintenance sum to be paid by the developer and for the ownership of the amenity open space involved to be conveyed to the authority."

An appendix to the circular makes special mention of parking provision. This states:

"1. Most developments require vehicle parking provision. Space for operational parking (eg service and delivery vehicles) will normally be expected to be provided on site. Subject to environmental, highway access, or traffic management considerations, the developer may also be required to provide appropriate non-operational parking on site. Planning conditions requiring a maximum or minimum number of spaces should be reasonable in relation to the size and nature of the development, the availability of public parking nearby, and local traffic management policies and parking standards. Consistency with local parking standards cannot be regarded as the sole test of the reasonableness of a planning condition.

2. Planning permission may be withheld if reasonable requirements as to the provision of parking spaces cannot practicably be met on site or on other land nearby under the control of the applicant, but to overcome such a valid objection the developer may agree to make a contribution to the provision of public parking spaces by the local authority. Such contributions may also be accepted when the developer could accommodate the required number of parking spaces on site, but would prefer not to do so. If a significant part of the use

is unconnected with the development, this may be reflected in the size of the developer's contribution. Payments should be no greater than is necessary to overcome a valid objection to planning permission or to commute a valid requirement and it follows that they should not be used to finance existing parking spaces or for purposes unrelated to the development."

The circular perhaps gives the stamp of legitimacy to planning gain, or to some forms of it. The circular provides, however, that if an applicant for planning permission considers suggested obligations to be unreasonable, he can appeal to the Secretary of State against a subsequent refusal of planning permission or the imposition of a condition; any such appeal will be considered in the light of the guidance given in the circular. Given the time which an appeal may take, this part of the circular may not have a great deal of impact.

Planning gain and the courts

Although agreements simply imply consensus between the parties, it is perhaps surprising, in view of the controversy aroused by the pursuit of planning gain that the subject has received such limited judicial scrutiny.

In *Re Abbey Homesteads (Developments) Application*[35] (*supra*) developers argued that an agreement conferred on a planning authority a planning gain which could not legitimately have been secured by a condition. They argued that the agreement was therefore *ultra vires* and unenforceable. However, it was not necessary for the Court of Appeal to deal with this issue.

In *City of Bradford Metropolitan Council* v. *Secretary of State for the Environment*[36] (see *supra*) a condition requiring road widening was held to be *ultra vires*. Lloyd L.J. went on to say, however, that "If the condition was manifestly unreasonable and so beyond the powers of the planning authority to impose it, it must follow that it was also beyond the powers of the planning authority to include the condition as 'an incidental or consequential provision' of an agreement restricting or regulating the development or use of land under section 52." A more limited agreement seeking a contribution towards the cost of road widening reflecting the increased use of the road resulting from the development and the benefit to the occupier of the development might have been acceptable. These remarks, although *obiter*, are of some importance as they lend support to the tests of reasonableness advanced in SDD Circular 22/1984 (see p. 140).

---

[35] (1985) 49 P. & C.R. 263.
[36] (1986) 53 P. & C.R. 55.

The only direct decision on the question of planning gain is that in *R. v. Gillingham Borough Council, ex p. F. Parham Ltd.*[37] (see Chapter 5). In that case, Roch J. upheld the validity of an agreement which required a developer to provide a road, not for the benefit of the proposed development but to facilitate the continuous and progressive development of neighbouring land. In doing so he concluded that a planning agreement could go beyond matters that fairly or reasonably related to the permitted development. Provided the agreement served a planning purpose and was not unreasonable in the sense of being irrational or promoted for some improper motive that was enough (see Chapter 5). Unless and until it is overturned, the decision in *Gillingham* may well be viewed by planning authorities as a green light to pursue planning gain. Furthermore, it would seem to place a very substantial question mark over the criterion of reasonableness set out in SDD Circular 22/1984 (see p. 144).

---

[37] [1988] J.P.L. 336.

CHAPTER 11

CONCLUSION

OUR recent survey shows a considerable increase in the use of
planning agreements in Scotland over the last six years. Their use
in the development control process is now widespread, if not yet
commonplace. It is reasonable to ask why this has happened and
what are the consequences. These are not questions which we
addressed in our survey so the answers must, to some extent at
least, remain a matter for conjecture. However, there are a number
of factors which seem likely to be relevant.

First of all, continuing restraint on public expenditure[1] has
meant that some local authority service departments have found
themselves less able to provide and maintain supporting infrastructure.[2] This has been most apparent with road improvements and
with the provision and maintenance of open space but is evident
also in other services. Planning agreements provide a vehicle for
redistributing the cost of provision and maintenance from the local
authority to the developer, a role which is recognised in SDD
Circular 22/1984 dealing with the use of agreements. This redistribution of costs has been especially apparent in growth areas such
as the Aberdeen area during the oil boom where infrastructure
capacity was under particular pressure. Although less pronounced,
this redistribution by way of agreement is becoming apparent in
other parts of Scotland as well.[3] Indeed, the use of agreements for
this purpose has got to the point where the Scottish Office may
soon have to review the way in which they tie in with the increasing
control of local authority capital expenditure. This is an area which
seems to be causing some confusion in the Department of the
Environment.[4]

Secondly, there seems little doubt that Circular 22/1984 has gone
a long way towards disposing of the feeling amongst some local
authorities that there was something "not quite right" about

---

[1] See H. Keating and R. Boyle, *Re-Making Urban Scotland* (Edinburgh University
Press, 1986), Ch. 4.
[2] See J. Rowan-Robinson and M. G. Lloyd, *Land Development and the Infrastructure Lottery*, (T. & T. Clark), 1988.
[3] *Ibid.*
[4] See *Estates Times*, April 29, 1988, p. 10.

bargaining in the development control process. The circular provides the official seal of approval to the practice. This has been supported by increasing recognition by reporters on appeal of the role of agreements in development control.[5]

Thirdly, local authority officers have, as a result of training courses, articles in journals and access to information about the experiences of other authorities, gained an increasing awareness of the potential of agreements; and the passage of time has given them greater familiarity and confidence with their practice.

Finally, the use of agreements provides planning authorities with considerable freedom from control by the SDD. Although few authorities acknowledged that the absence of a right of appeal to the Secretary of State was an important factor in their use, our impression is that there is some unhappiness amongst authorities over the gradual shift in power which has occurred in the development control process over the last few years from local to central government as a result of the latter's determination to "release the spirit of enterprise."[6] Whilst many authorities are equally keen to promote enterprise, they prefer to be in a position to control its social consequences. The use of agreements affords them that control.

These four factors seem likely to have influenced the increasing use of agreements in Scotland. This increasing use has yet to attract the attention of the courts in Scotland although agreements have now come under judicial scrutiny in England. There is no doubt that the attitude of the courts to the use of agreements will have an important bearing on practice. However, Lloyd L. J.'s somewhat ominous observation in *City of Bradford Metropolitan Council* v. *Secretary of State for the Environment*[7] that "the practice under section 52, convenient and beneficial though it undoubtedly is, may have gone beyond what the strict language of the section justifies" has yet to manifest itself in clear guidance as to the limits of bargaining in development control. In *Avon County Council* v. *Millard*[8] the Court of Appeal in considering the question of remedies for the breach of a planning agreement were prepared to treat it as a contract between parties. Uncertainty has, however, arisen as to how far public law concepts may be relevant to the contractual process given that one of the parties to the contract is a public body acting under statutory powers. The decisions in

[5] See, *e.g.* SPADS Nos. A 3253, A 5639, A 5461, A 5667.
[6] See, generally, Cmnd. 9571, "Lifting the Burden" (HMSO, July 1985) and Cmnd. 9794, "Building Businesses . . . Not Barriers" (HMSO, May 1986).
[7] (1986) 53 P. & C.R. 55.
[8] (1985) 274 E.G. 1025. See *supra*.

Windsor and Maidenhead Royal Borough Council v. *Brandrose Investments*[9] on fettering discretionary powers and in *R.* v. *Gillingham Borough Council, ex p. F. Parham Ltd.*[10] on the exercise of discretionary powers have done little to resolve this uncertainty. It would seem that the courts, like others, find difficulty in reconciling a private contractual relationship with a public regulatory process.

The consequences of the increasing use of agreements in Scotland are more difficult to determine. There has, however, been no outcry by developers about their use. The reponse by the building industry to the draft of what eventually became SDD Circular 22/1984 was not one of hostility to the bargaining process but rather that the proposed tests of reasonableness were likely to be helpful. Neither has there been a spate of appeals against refusals of planning permission consequent on rejection of an agreement, though this may simply reflect the ability of planning authorities to support such a refusal on conventional planning grounds or, more likely, the judgment of the developer that the cost of assuming the obligations in the agreement will be less than the time, expense and uncertainty involved in an appeal.[11] Developers, in many cases, are able in any event to offset the costs of the agreement against the price for the land or, alternatively, to pass them forward to the consumer. Only exceptionally, it seems, does a proposal for an agreement result in the developer walking away from a scheme.[12]

There are also indications that agreements are, in the words of Lloyd L. J. "convenient and beneficial." They are helpful to both the planning authority and the developer in smoothing the path to a grant of planning permission. And many planning authorities in Scotland, it should be said, particularly in areas of physical and economic decline, are anxious to secure development in their areas. Setting aside for the moment questions of planning gain, and our survey indicates that the great majority of agreements in Scotland are not concerned with the pursuit of planning gain in the sense of securing benefits extraneous to the development, most of the agreements that we have seen have been concerned with removing obstacles to a grant of planning permission which cannot be dealt with by condition, or with providing planning authorities with a more flexible and readily enforceable instrument of control

---

[9] [1981] 1 W.L.R. 1083; [1983] 1 W.L.R. 509 (C.A.). See Chap. 6.
[10] [1988] J.P.L. 336. See Chap. 5.
[11] J. Rowan-Robinson and M. G. Lloyd, *Land Development and the Infrastructure Lottery, supra*, Chap. 6.
[12] *Ibid.*

than conditions. They are, in other words, a vehicle for helping development to happen.

It is in our view unfortunate that the very real benefits for the land development process which may be obtained through the use of planning agreements are often obscured by debate about the more emotive topic of planning gain. The pursuit of planning gain does, as we have indicated in Chapter 10, raise important issues which require to be addressed. But these issues are of a different order to those with which we have been principally concerned in this book. The great majority of agreements in Scotland serve a supplementary development control function and we think it important that any discussion about the role of agreements and the need for constraint on their use in Scotland should recognise this. The pursuit of planning gain is, as yet, a relatively minor issue. Indeed, it seems to us that SDD Circular 22/1984 which is concerned for the most part with discouraging the pursuit of extraneous gains is addressing what appears to be much more of an English problem. This is not to suggest that the use of agreements in Scotland should be free from scrutiny and guidance, but rather that they should be seen for what they essentially are, a useful supplement to the development control powers of planning authorities.

Having said that, we cannot, of course, ignore our finding that the use of agreements to secure extraneous gains, although relatively limited, is on the increase in Scotland. Whether we will see an upsurge in their use such as appears to have occurred in England seems doubtful. Although the factors underlying this upsurge are not well researched, the pursuit of planning gain seems to be linked to growth. Given the general uncertainty which surrounds land development in much of Scotland, the incidence of planning gain has been confined for the most part to large retailing proposals.

The question remains, however, whether the pursuit of extraneous gains is an acceptable practice. If that question is addressed simply in the context of the legislation presently governing the development control process, we are inclined to think that there is no place for the pursuit of such gains. Although there are inevitably problems at the margin in determining what is "extraneous", we think, to borrow the words of one commentator, that "the prospect of such rewards does not exactly encourage cool and disinterested judgement"[13] of individual proposals for develop-

---

[13] Peter Shore, M.P., quoted in the *Estates Times* (May 20, 1988) in connection with the proposed development of Spitalfields Market in London.

ment. We do not think, as we mentioned in Chapter 5, that an extraneous gain can be said to be relevant to the decision on the planning application. In other words where a section 50 agreement is linked to a planning application, and it nearly always is, the agreement is intended to supplement the development control process; it is not supposed to be an instrument for taxing development licences. This is a matter of interpretation and one, of course, which rests ultimately with the courts. While we recognise that our view is to some extent inconsistent with the decision in *Gillingham*, that decision is not binding on the Scottish courts. Although judicial attitudes are not as homogenous as is sometimes suggested, some Scottish judges, particularly the members of the First Division, have shown themselves especially concerned to protect private rights—often to a greater extent than seems evident in England.[14] It may be, therefore, that the decision of Roch J. in *Gillingham* would not find support in Scotland.

If, however, the question whether the pursuit of extraneous gains is an acceptable practice is addressed in terms of whether the planning system should be changed, that is a very different matter. Should we, for example, as Mather has recently suggested, be formalising the pursuit of planning gain by allowing planning authorities to sell or auction planning consents?[15] Some of the arguments for and against the use of this sort of pricing mechanism are discussed in Chapter 10. We think this a subject which in the present economic and political climate is likely to attract continuing attention. However, interesting as it is, it is not a matter on which we feel it is appropriate at this point to offer a view. It raises questions about the market economy, the role of the state and the place of town and country planning which are beyond the scope of this book. Our concern has been more mundanely, with the legislation presently governing the development control process and, in particular, with section 50 and the way in which it has been interpreted and employed in practice.

[14] See E. Young and J. Rowan-Robinson, "Development Control in Scotland" in *Planning Control: Philosophies, Prospects and Practice*, M. L. Harrison and R. Mordey (eds.), (Croom Helm, 1987).
[15] G. Mather, "Pricing for Planning" (Institute of Economic Affairs, March 1988).

TOWN AND COUNTRY PLANNING (SCOTLAND) ACT 1972, s. 50

(1) A planning authority may enter into an agreement with any person interested in land in their area (in so far as the interest of that person enables him to bind the land) for the purpose of restricting or regulating the development or use of the land, either permanently or during such period as may be prescribed by the agreement: and any such agreement may contain such incidental and consequential provisions (including provisions of a financial character) as appear to the planning authority to be necessary or expedient for the purposes of the agreement.

(2) An agreement made under this section with any person interested in land, may, if the agreement shall have been recorded in the appropriate Register of Sasines, be enforceable at the instance of the planning authority against persons deriving title to the land from the person with whom the agreement was entered into:

Provided that no such agreement shall at any time be enforceable against a third party who shall have in bona fide onerously acquired right (whether completed by infeftment or not) to the land prior to the agreement being recorded as aforesaid or against any person deriving title from such third party.

(3) Nothing in this section or in any agreement made thereunder shall be construed—

(a) as restricting the exercise, in relation to land which is the subject of any such agreement, of any powers exercisable by any Minister or authority under this Act so long as those powers are exercised in accordance with the provisions of the development plan, or in accordance with any directions which may have been given by the Secretary of State as to the provisions to be included in such a plan, or

(b) as requiring the exercise of any such powers otherwise than as mentioned in paragraph (a) of this subsection.

*(4) In this section "planning authority" includes a regional planning authority.

---

* This subsection was added by the Local Government and Planning (Scotland) Act 1982 (see Sched. 2, para. 14).

SCOTTISH DEVELOPMENT DEPARTMENT CIRCULAR
No. 22/1984

To: The Chief Executive   New St Andrew's House
Regional and Islands Councils   Edinburgh, EH1 3SZ.
The Chief Executive   Tel. 031-556 8400.
District Councils
(except in Highland, Borders and Dumfries
and Galloway Regions)   3 August 1984

Dear Sir

TOWN AND COUNTRY PLANNING (SCOTLAND) ACT 1972 SECTION 50 AGREEMENTS

1. The purpose of this Circular is to give guidance to regional, general and district planning authorities on the circumstances in which they might wish to impose obligations on developers and others with an interest in land in their area; and in particular to give guidance on the making—in connection with, or unrelated to, applications for planning permission—of agreements under section 50 of the Town and Country Planning (Scotland) Act 1972.

Background

2. It is a matter of law as well as of good administration that planning applications must be considered on their planning merits, having regard to the provisions of the development plan and any other material consideration. They should be refused only when this serves a clear planning purpose. By the same token, the question of imposing a condition or obligation—whether negative or positive in character—should arise only where it is considered that it would not be appropriate to grant permission in the terms sought which is not subject to such a condition or obligation.

3. If a planning application is considered in this light, a planning authority may find themselves in the position of having to refuse the application in the following circumstances (which are intended to be illustrative rather than exhaustive):

140

(a) because a valid or effective planning condition cannot be imposed, *e.g.* to require works to be carried out on land not included in the site of the development for which planning permission has been requested although an assurance that such works will be carried out would be essential before planning permission could be granted: or

(b) because of the adverse effects that the proposed development would have on the surrounding area which could be overcome only by the carrying out of public or private bodies of infrastructure works such as road improvement schemes or additional car parking provision, but which may not be undertaken by these bodies because of financial constraints or competing priorities; or

(c) because a condition required in any grant of planning permission would not be capable of enforcement against successors in title of the developers; or

(d) because the proposed development would be incompatible with an existing grant of planning permission for a development on an adjacent site.

4. This situation is clearly distinguishable from the case in which the planning authority are endeavouring to secure alterations or modifications to a proposed development in the course of their consideration of the planning application, *e.g.* a change intended to reduce the scale or intensity of the proposed development or to improve its layout or its impact on the local environment.

5. Where a condition would be difficult to enforce in practice or inadequate or inappropriate, an agreement under section 50 freely entered into may be appropriate to enable the original development to proceed. In some cases the developer may offer to carry out some works or make some payment either when applying for planning permission or in the course of subsequent negotiations with the planning authority in order to overcome a difficulty in securing the grant of planning permission. The guidance in this Circular is relevant to those circumstances as well as to cases where the authority take the initiative. It will be noted that this Circular is not concerned with the case where the authority are disposing of land which they own and where the terms and conditions on which they are prepared to sell are matters for negotiation with prospective purchasers, nor is it concerned with matters arising from other legislative provisions, *e.g.* the acquisition, by agreement or compulsorily, of rights in connection with the provision of a water supply or the laying of a public sewer.

Legal aspects
6. The scope for using conditional planning permissions under

Part III of the Town and Country Planning (Scotland) Act 1972 for the purpose of imposing obligations on developers is subject to the limitations that any conditions must achieve a proper planning purpose, be relevant to the development authorised by the permission and be reasonable in other respects.

7. As regards agreements, the powers which are given to regional, general and district planning authorities under section 50 of the 1972 Act are to enter into agreements with persons having an interest in land in their area (insofar as the interest of the person concerned enables him to bind the land) for the purpose of "restricting or regulating the development or use of the land." (Paragraph 14 of Schedule 2 to the Local Government and Planning (Scotland) Act 1982 extended the definition of planning authority to regional planning authority, for the purposes of section 50.) One of the main advantages of using section 50 is that provisions in such agreements are, by virtue of subsection (2), enforceable by the planning authority against successors in title of the person or body who entered into the agreement if the agreement has been recorded in the appropriate Register of Sasines or registered in accordance with the Land Registration (Scotland) Act 1979, as appropriate. Moreover, such agreements need not be associated with a specific grant of planning permission but may also in appropriate cases modify the conditions or limitations in such a grant.

8. Only a person whose interest at the time of signing the agreement enables him to bind the land may enter into a section 50 agreement, namely, the person whose name appears on the Register as the owner or the lessee under a record lease. A person whose only interest is that of developer or prospective purchaser may not enter into such agreements.

9. As to the question of whether an obligation of a positive nature can be imposed by way of a section 50 agreement, such agreements are "for the purpose of restricting or regulating the development or use of the land." While these words suggest a restrictive connotation, by taking a broad view of the purpose of the development proposed as a whole the inclusion of such obligations on the basis that their underlying overall purpose is restrictive in regulating the development itself may be justified. Such obligations might relate to the provision of car parking or open space (see paragraph 14 below), or might provide for housing as part of an office development, or secure the retention or restoration of a building which is of architectural or historical importance, but is not listed. Incidental and consequential provisions (including provisions of a financial character) which are

considered necessary or expedient for the purposes of the agreement may also be included.

10. In addition to the power to enter into such agreements, local authorities have a general power to make agreements with developers under section 69 of the Local Government (Scotland) Act 1973. It gives them power "to do anything (whether or not involving the expenditure, borrowing or lending of money or the acquisition or disposal of any property or rights) which is calculated to facilitate, or is conducive or incidental to, the discharge of their functions." The section would, for example, enable agreements to be made, which would not have to be limited in their purpose to restricting or regulating the development or use of land, for the payment of money or the transfer of assets to a local authority where this would facilitate the discharge of the functions of the authority. The section does not empower the local authority to require such a transfer; the transfer must be by agreement. However unlike recorded or registered agreements made under section 50 of the 1972 Act, such agreements would normally be enforceable only against the person or body with whom they were made.

General policy on agreements under section 50

11. In considering the use of the power to conclude an agreement under section 50, a planning authority should have regard to the extent to which the agreement will assist in securing the best use of land and a properly planned environment. The following paragraphs give guidance as to how these objectives may be achieved.

12. Where the planning authority and a developer who wishes to apply for planning permission have concluded that a section 50 agreement should be made between them, but the developer does not at that time have an interest which enables him to bind the land because he does not have a recorded title, a registered interest or a recorded lease, the planning authority should, where appropriate, consider giving the developer an indication that planning permission will be forthcoming if the section 50 agreement is duly entered into and recorded or registered. This will enable the developer to conclude missives and record his title, register his interest or record the lease, as appropriate, and thereafter to enter into the section 50 agreement with the planning authority. The planning permission should be granted after the agreement has been entered into and recorded or registered.

13. This does not mean that an authority is entitled to treat an applicant's need for permission as an opportunity to obtain some

extraneous benefit or advantage or as an opportunity to exact a payment for the benefit of ratepayers at large. Nor should the preparation of such an agreement be permitted to delay unduly the decision on the application.

14. The test of the reasonableness of imposing such obligations on developers depends substantially on whether what is required:

(1) is needed to enable the development to go ahead, *e.g.* provision of adequate access, water supply and sewerage and sewage disposal facilities; or

(2) in case of financial payments, will contribute to meeting the cost of providing such facilities in the near future; or

(3) is otherwise so directly related to the proposed development and to the use of the land after its completion that the development ought not to be permitted without it, *e.g.* the provision, whether by the developer or by the authority at the developer's expense, of car parking in or near the development or reasonable amounts of open space related to the development; or

(4) is designed in the case of mixed development to secure an acceptable balance of uses.

The Appendix to this Circular illustrates the application of these general principles to the provision of car parking. Section 50 agreements might also cover complicated technical matters such as the operation of an oil refinery, or cover arrangements to enable archaeological investigations to be carried out before or during the development.

15. If what is required or sought passes one of the tests set out in the preceding paragraph, a further test has to be applied. This is whether the extent of what is required or sought is fairly and reasonably related in scale and kind to the proposed development. Thus while the developer may reasonably be expected to pay for or contribute to the cost of infrastructure which would not have been necessary but for his development, and while some public benefit may eventually accrue from this, his payments should be directly related in scale and kind to the benefit which the proposed development will derive from the facilities to be provided.

16. There is also a final test, namely whether what the developer is being asked to provide or help to finance represents in itself a reasonable charge on the developer as distinct from being financed by national or local taxation or other means—*e.g.* as a charge on those using the facility provided. The essential principle to apply is that the facility to be provided or financed should be directly related to the development in question or the use of the land after development. It would not normally be reasonable, for example, to seek a contribution to road construction or improvement in the

immediate vicinity of the proposed development unless the need for this arises wholly or substantially from the new development.

Minerals
17. Those general considerations hold good in their application to mineral development. As explained in SDD Circular 5/1982, the Town and Country Planning (Minerals) Act 1981 provides specific powers for a planning authority to add aftercare conditions to minerals planning permissions where the land is to be reclaimed for agricultural, forestry or amenity use. There are also provisions which have not yet been brought into effect relating to the review of existing workings and, under certain circumstances, the imposition of up to date conditions. Even when these new powers are available, there will be occasions when agreements between planning authority and developer will be appropriate, or where an agreement in advance of planning consent is the only way of achieving certain preliminary works (for example improvements to sight lines at road junctions). It is also hoped that planning authorities and developers will continue to enter into voluntary agreements to achieve environmental improvements where both sides recognise that existing planning conditions are inadequate or inappropriate. Such agreements reflect the greater sensitivity towards environmental needs that has developed in recent years, and in particular an awareness by both the industry and planning authorities of the need for the restoration of land previously worked but left unrestored for lack of satisfactory conditions requiring works to be carried out for this purpose. Advice will be given when the 1981 Act is brought fully into effect on how the cost to developers of undertaking such voluntary works might be taken into account in the compensation calculation which would follow the subsequent imposition of new conditions.

Provision of public access
18. Where the developer provides space or other facilities, *e.g.* amenity walkways, he cannot be required to dedicate these to the public (though he may volunteer such an arrangement). If authorities think general public access appropriate, and the developer does not wish to provide it, it is for them to seek acquisition of the necessary rights in the land. If the developer is willing to donate the 'land to a third party that party should be involved in the discussions at the earliest possible stage.

Maintenance payments
19. The issue has arisen whether, in addition to providing

facilities such as open space or contributing to their capital costs, developers should also be expected to pay towards their maintenance costs. Where such facilities are of general public benefit the developer may be willing to dedicate them to the public. In such cases the developer's responsibility should be limited to providing what is needed in the first instance and all costs of subsequent maintenance should normally be borne by the authority or body in which the asset is to be vested. However, in smaller scale developments, such as housing estates, open areas of grass or landscaping are principally of benefit to the development itself rather than to the wider public and the developer can reasonably be expected to make suitable provision for subsequent maintenance. This may not be a matter which can be dealt with effectively by means of a planning condition. In appropriate circumstances, authorities may, therefore, wish to discuss the issue with prospective developers with a view to securing an agreement on maintenance arrangements. Such an agreement might, for instance, provide for a suitable commuted maintenance sum to be paid by the developer and for the ownership of the amenity open space involved to be conveyed to the authority.

Cases involving other land or buildings

20. Obligations imposed on developers may reasonably affect land other than that covered by the planning permission provided that there is a direct relationship between the two. For example permission might be given for a new building where the developer is willing to agree to demolish a nearby building, the rationale of this being that the impact of the new building would be offset by the environmental improvement resulting from removal of the existing building. Similarly, it might be appropriate to seek the restoration of a nearby building as a screen for the new building. However it would not be appropriate to seek to require the demolition of a building which is unrelated to the proposed development. As described in paragraph 14 above and the Appendix to this Circular, a section 50 agreement might also cover the provision of, or a contribution to the cost of providing, a car park at a site separate from that of the proposed development, but such an agreement would be appropriate only if the proposed car park was near to, and required, either wholly or in part, for the support of the development in question.

Development plans and appeals

21. Where planning authorities intend to seek to impose obligations which meet the tests set out in this Circular, they should,

where appropriate, provide guidance to this effect in development plans. Should authorities seek to impose obligations in connection with a grant of planning permission the applicant may refuse to accept them because he considers them to be unreasonable and appeal to the Secretary of State against a subsequent refusal of permission or imposition of a condition, or the non-determination of the application. Such appeals will be considered in the light of the advice given in this Circular.

22. Further copies of this Circular can be obtained from Mr I. Rutherford (Ext. 5372) and any enquiries should be addressed to Mr C. M. A. Lugton (Ext. 4631).

Yours faithfully
D. J. ESSERY

PARKING PROVISION   APPENDIX

1. Most developments require vehicle parking provision. Space for operational parking (*e.g.* service and delivery vehicles) will normally be expected to be provided on site. Subject to environmental, highway access, or traffic management considerations, the developer may also be required to provide appropriate non-operational parking on site. Planning conditions requiring a maximum or minimum number of spaces should be reasonable in relation to the size and nature of the development, the availability of public parking nearby, and local traffic management policies and parking standards. Consistency with local parking standards cannot be regarded as the sole test of the reasonableness of a planning condition. The reasonableness of the standards themselves may be open to question on appeal against refusal of permission. Authorities should not include excessive requirements in parking standards in order to increase their income from commuted payments.

2. Planning permission may be withheld if reasonable requirements as to the provision of parking spaces cannot practicably be met on site or on other land nearby under the control of the applicant, but to overcome such a valid objection the developer may agree to make a contribution to the provision of public parking spaces by the local authority. Such contributions may also be accepted when the developer could accommodate the required number of parking spaces on site, but would prefer not to do so. Whether the agreement is to overcome a valid objection to planning permission, or to commute a valid planning condition, the parking spaces provided should be easily accessible and convenient to the application site, and should be provided within a reasonable time. If a significant part of the use is unconnected

with the development, this may be reflected in the size of the developer's contribution. Payments should be no greater than is necessary to overcome a valid objection to planning permission or to commute a valid requirement and it follows that they should not be used to finance existing parking spaces or for purposes unrelated to the development.

3. Similar tests should apply where planning authorities have made it a deliberate policy to restrict non-operational parking in order to discourage car commuting or to reduce car use in environmentally sensitive areas. Where the provision of parking away from the site arises from such policies, rather than the developer's preference or the limitations of the application site, the principle still applies that the developer's contribution should be used only to increase the existing provision, and that the spaces provided should be as convenient as possible to the users of the development, and reasonable in relation to its size and nature and to the local authority's parking standards. The test of proximity to the development may be relaxed in park and ride or pedestrianisation schemes. The key test is again that payments should be put to a use which overcomes a valid objection to planning permission.

APPENDIX 3

BIBLIOGRAPHY

J. F. Garner, "Agreements Under Section 25" [1949] J.P.L. 628.

M. Grant, "Planning by Agreement" [1975] J.P.L. 501.

A. Levings, "Planning by Agreement—the *Beaconsfield* Case" [1975] J.P.L. 704.

H. W. Clarke, "Enforceability of Development Agreements" (1975) 125 New L.J. 651.

M. Aves, "Enforcing Section 52 Agreements" [1976] J.P.L. 216 and 262.

J. Jowell, "Bargaining in Development Control" [1977] J.P.L. 414.

J. Jowell, "The Limits of the Law in Urban Planning" (1977) 30 C.L.P. 64.

R. N. D. Hamilton, "Drafting Planning Agreements" [1977] L.G.C. 739.

M. Grant, "Developers' Contributions and Planning Gain: Ethics and Legalities" [1978] J.P.L. 8.

M. Loughlin, "Bargaining as a Tool of Development Control: A Case of All Gain and No Loss" [1978] J.P.L. 290.

A. Samuels, "Planning Agreements: Their Use and Misuse" [1978] L.G. Rev. 609 and 624.

L. R. Tucker, "Planning Agreements: The Twilight Zone of Ultra Vires" [1978] J.P.L. 806.

R. W. Suddards, "Section 52 Agreements: A Case for New Legislation" [1979] J.P.L. 661.

J. N. Hawke, "Section 52 Agreements and the Fettering of Planning Powers" [1980] J.P.L. 386.

Sir D. Heap and A. J. Ward, "Planning Bargaining: The Pros and the Cons: or How Much Can the System Stand?" [1980] J.P.L. 631.

J. N. Hawke, "Planning Agreements in Practice" [1981] J.P.L. 5 and 86.

A. J. Ward, "Planning Agreements and the March of Time: Removing Obsolete Restrictions" [1981] J.P.L. 557.

J. Ratcliffe, "Planning Gain—An Overview" (1981) 258 E.G. 407.

M. Loughlin, "Planning Gain: Law, Policy and Practice" (1981) 1 Ox.Jo. L.S. 61.

A. Davies, "Planning Bargaining and Planning Gain", *Guardian Gazette*, 2 December 1981, p.1366.

F. J. Reade, "Section 52 and Corporatism in Planning" [1982] J.P.L. 8.

A. J. Ward, "Planning Bargaining: Where Do We Stand?" [1982] J.P.L. 74.

L. Durrant, "Planning Gain—How Development Can Pay For a By-Pass", *Chartered Surveyor*, February 1982, p.396.

J. Jowell, "Giving Planning Gain a Bad Name" [1982] L.G.C. 155.

M. Grant, "False Diagnosis, Wrong Prescription", *Town and Country Planning*, March 1982, p.38.

M. Loughlin, "Planning Gain: Another Viewpoint" [1982] J.P.L. 352.

D. J. M. Wilson, "Planning Gain and Office Development: Policy and Practice" (1982) 262 E.G. 301.

Royal Institution of Chartered Surveyors, *An Approach to Planning Gains*, 8 May 1981.

Property Advisory Group, *Planning Gain*, H.M.S.O., 1981.

149

Royal Town Planning Institute, *Planning Gain*, comments on the report by the Property Advisory Group, 28 January 1982.

The Law Society, "Planning Gain: The Law Society's Observations" [1982] J.P.L. 346.

J. Jowell and M. Grant, "A Critical Look at Planning Gain" (1983) 147 L.G.R. 491.

J. Jowell and M. Grant, "Guidelines for Planning Gain?" [1983] J.P.L. 427.

E. Young and J. Rowan-Robinson, "Section 52 Agreements and the Fettering of Powers" [1982] J.P.L. 673.

R. N. D. Hamilton, "Planning Agreements" (1983) 127 Sol. Jo. 568 and 588.

Royal Town Planning Institute, "Planning Gain Guidelines", observations submitted to the Department of Environment, April 1983.

M. Grant, "The Planning After Effects of the *Brandrose* Litigation" [1983] L.G.C. 768.

A. Ward, "Planning Agreements: For Better or Worse?" (1984) 134 New L.J. 905.

D. W. Cockburn, "Section 50 Agreements: Some Aspects for the Conveyancer" (1984) 12 S.P.L.P. 38.

R. R. Spinney, "Planning Gain—A Developer's View" (in J.P.E.L. Occasional Paper, *Contemporary Planning Policies*, Sweet and Maxwell, 1984).

"Section 50 Agreements", report by the Society of Directors of Administration, (1984) 12 S.P.L.P. 40.

S. M. Nott and P. H. Morgan, "Section 52 Agreements–Not Worth The Paper They Are Written On?" (1984) 269 E.G. 476.

J. A. Spens, "Section 50 Agreements: Procedural Provisions" (1985) 15 S.P.L.P. 41.

P. F. Smith. "Some Recent Problems with Section 52 Agreements" (1986) 136 New L.J. 1144.

R. N. D. Hamilton, "Drafting Planning Agreements" (1987) 131 So. Jo. 34.

J.P.E.L. Occasional paper, *Development Control—Thirty Years On* (1979) papers 2, 3 and 4.

Blundell Memorial Lecture 1981, "Planning Gain: How is this Form of Plea Bargaining Justified?".

J. Douglas Cramond, "Planning by Agreement" (unpublished B.Sc. research essay, Department of Town and Country Planning, Heriot-Watt University, 1979).

Isabel Bruce, "Section 50 Agreements" (unpublished Diploma thesis, Department of Urban and Regional Planning, University of Strathclyde, 1979).

International Bar Association, *Planning Law for Industry* (1981).

I. Simpson, "Planning Gain" in *Planning Control: Philosophies, Prospects and Practice*, chap. 6 (eds. M. L. Harrison and R. Mordey, Croom Helm, 1987).

J. Alder, *Development Control* (1979), chap 6.

J. Ratcliffe, *Land Policy*, pp.86–88.

M. Purdue, *Cases and Materials on Planning Law* (1977), pp.363–367.

J. M. Evans, *de Smith's Judicial Review of Administrative Action* (4th ed., 1980) pp.317 *et. seq.*

H. W. R. Wade, *Administrative Law* (6th ed., 1988), pp.787–790.

R.I.C.S. Practice Note No. 4 (Scotland), *Section 50 Agreements* (1981).

C. Turpin, *Government Contracts* (1972).

M. Grant, *Urban Planning Law*, Sweet and Maxwell (1982), and First Supplement (1986).

G. Mather, "Pricing for Planning", Institute for Economic Affairs, March 1988.

INDEX

Access agreements, 92, 103–106
  area access, 104–105
  linear access, 105–106
Agreements
  access. See Access agreements.
  environmentally sensitive areas. See
    Environmentally Sensitive
    Areas.
  forestry dedication agreement. See
    Forestry.
  general power to contract, 3, 6, 9,
    43–56, 93, 94–95, 143
  inheritance tax exemption. See
    Inheritance tax.
  long distance footpaths. See
    Footpaths.
  nature reserves. See Nature reserves.
  National Trust for Scotland,
    conservation agreements. See
    National Trust for Scotland.
  public path creation agreements. See
    Footpaths.
  scenic and recreational agreements.
    See Scenic and recreational
    agreements.
  sites of special scientific interest. See
    Sites of special scientific
    interest.
  section 50 agreements. See Section
    50 agreements.
  section 52 agreements. See Section
    52 agreements.
Appeals
  influence of agreements on appeal
    decisions, 57, 58, 59, 60, 70
  in the event of failure to agree, 9,
    126, 136, 147

Car parking, 78, 84, 85, 90, 123, 131–
  132, 142, 144, 146, 147
Circulars
  imposition of conditions on planning
    permissions, 59–60, 74, 75, 76,
    77, 78–79, 80, 84, 128–129
  planning gain, 39–40, 113, 128–132
  use of agreements, 1, 25, 27, 28, 36,
    60, 85, 90, 94, 128–132, 134,
    136, 137, 140–148

Compensation
  restriction on existing use rights, 86,
    92
Covenants
  positive, 18–20
  restrictive, 18–20
Conditions. See Planning permission.
Countryside
  access agreements. See Access
    agreements.
  environmentally sensitive areas. See
    Environmentally sensitive
    areas.
  footpaths. See Footpaths.
  forestry. See Forestry.
  inheritance tax exemption. See
    Inheritance tax.
  nature reserves. See Nature reserves.
  scenic and recreational agreements.
    See Scenic and recreational
    agreements.
  sites of special scientific interest. See
    Sites of special scientific
    interest.
Countryside Commission for Scotland
  inheritance tax exemption, 11
  long distance footpaths. See
    Footpaths.
  power to enter into agreements, 23,
    102–103, 106

Definitions
  material considerations, 34
  planning gain, 8, 90, 112–113, 121
Department of Agriculture and
    Fisheries for Scotland, 9, 92, 107
  environmentally sensitive areas. See
    Environmentally sensitive
    areas.
Development control
  agreements as supplement to, 1, 7,
    8, 33, 136–137
  Link with agreements, 1, 6, 7, 25, 30,
    42, 57–62, 90, 138
  material considerations, 34–38
Development plans, 35, 122, 139, 140,
  146–147
Discontinuance order, 86